MAKING NATURE'S CITY
A science-based framework for building urban biodiversity

PREPARED BY SFEI   Erica Spotswood
Robin Grossinger
Steve Hagerty
Micaela Bazo
Matthew Benjamin
Erin Beller
Letitia Grenier
Ruth Askevold

SFEI | San Francisco
Estuary Institute

SFEI PUBLICATION #947
September 2019

A product of the Healthy Watersheds, Resilient Baylands project
Funded by the San Francisco Bay Water Quality Improvement Fund, EPA Region IX,
with additional funding from the Google Ecology Program and the Peninsula Open Space Trust

SUGGESTED CITATION

San Francisco Estuary Institute. 2019. Making Nature's City: A science-based framework for building urban biodiversity. A product of the Healthy Watersheds, Resilient Baylands project. Funded by the San Francisco Bay Water Quality Improvement Fund, EPA Region IX. SFEI Publication #947, San Francisco Estuary Institute, Richmond, CA.

VERSION

v. 1.1 (September, 2019)

REPORT AVAILABILITY

Report is available online at www.sfei.org

COVER IMAGE CREDITS

Cover flora and fauna courtesy of the Biodiversity Heritage Library.

CONTENTS

Acknowledgements

The Urban Biodiversity Framework is part of the *Healthy Watersheds, Resilient Baylands* project, which is funded by a grant to the San Francisco Estuary Partnership from the San Francisco Bay Water Quality Improvement Fund of the US Environmental Protection Agency Region IX. The report also received additional funding from the Google Ecology Program and the Peninsula Open Space Trust.

We are deeply grateful to the members of the technical advisory committee for their guidance, technical advice, and enthusiastic contributions to the project: Myla Aronson (Rutgers University), Alex Felson (Connecticut Institute for Resilience and Climate Adaptation, University of Connecticut), Peter Groffman (Cary Institute of Ecosystem Studies, The City University of New York), Nicole Heller (Carnegie Museum of Natural History), and Claire Kremen (University of British Columbia).

We would like to thank Luisa Valiela (EPA) for her invaluable guidance and support throughout the project. We are also grateful for technical advice, review, and support provided by Darcie Luce and Caitlin Sweeney (San Francisco Estuary Partnership); Michelle Daher (City of East Palo Alto); Elaine Marshall, Melody Tovar, and Michelle King (City of Sunnyvale); Catherine Martineau, Elise Willis, and Michael Hawkins (Canopy); Kate Randolph, Ashley Muse, Audrey Davenport, and Kate Malmgrem (Google); Alex Von Feldt, Junko Bryant, and Claire Elliott (Grassroots Ecology); Steve Rottenborn, Dan Stephens and Rachel Visscher (H.T. Harvey & Associates); Andrea Mackenzie, Marc Landgraf, and Matt Freeman (Santa Clara Valley Open Space Authority). This project has also benefited greatly from interactions with Google staff and design teams in applying the framework to the Google campus in Mountain View.

Additional thanks go to interns Megan Wheeler (Arizona State University) and Nick Mascarello (The Bill Lane Center for the American West at Stanford University) for analysis, advising, and help with writing. Finally, we are grateful to the many SFEI-ASC staff members who contributed to this project, including Shira Bezalel, Katie McKnight, Amy Richey, Micha Salomon, Sam Safran, April Robinson, Pete Kauhanen, Gloria Desanker, Julie Beagle, Sean Baumgarten, Emily Clark, and Jen Hunt. §

ABSTRACT

Cities will face many challenges over the coming decades, from adapting to a changing climate to accommodating rapid population growth. A related suite of challenges threatens global biodiversity, and many species face potential extinction. While urban planners and conservationists have long treated these issues as distinct, there is growing evidence that cities not only harbor a significant fraction of the world's biodiversity, but that they can also be made more livable and resilient for people, plants, and animals through nature-friendly urban design.

Urban ecological science can provide a powerful tool to guide cities towards more biodiversity-friendly design. However, current research remains scattered across thousands of journal articles and largely inaccessible to practitioners. *Making Nature's City* fills this gap, synthesizing global research to develop a science-based approach for supporting nature in cities. We identify seven key elements of urban form and function that work together to maximize biodiversity, and we illustrate these elements through a case study in California's Silicon Valley.

Using the framework developed in this report, urban designers and local residents can work together to link local parks, greenways, green roofs, street trees, stormwater basins, commercial landscaping, and backyards to support biodiversity while making cities better places to live. As we envision the healthier, and more resilient cities, *Making Nature's City* provides practical guidance for the many actors who together will shape the nature of cities. §

1

INTRODUCTION

Why biodiversity in the city?

Protecting biodiversity is central to global conservation and human well-being. In cities, nature can regulate flooding, mitigate water pollution, and capture carbon from the atmosphere. Urban nature can also improve human health by reducing air pollution and exposure to extreme heat, promoting active lifestyles, and improving psychological well-being. While small numbers of plant species can provide some of these services, biodiverse nature can substantially improve the benefits that people derive from nature (Sandifer et al. 2015). Protecting and enhancing biodiversity in cities is critical for creating spaces where people can thrive, and where urban habitat and stewardship can support regional conservation goals.

Over the coming decades, many cities will undergo a transformation. Some will face increasing pressure to develop as people move to centers of economic opportunity, while others will shrink. All cities will face pressure to adapt to a changing climate and many will need to accommodate rising sea levels, increased flood risk, and higher temperatures. As these changes occur, we have the opportunity to incorporate ecologically-friendly design and to strategically plan for the promotion and protection of greenspace in a way that maximizes biodiversity. Achieving this objective will require coordinated planning that is informed by science, and that places a priority on enhancing urban biodiversity.

Creating vibrant ecological cities that incorporate nature will not only support biodiversity, but will also make a profound contribution to the quality of life of urban residents. Respiratory illnesses linked to air pollution, heat exposure from urban heat islands, and obesity and hypertension fueled by sedentary lifestyles are some examples of how cities can negatively affect people. Incorporating nature as a valued type of infrastructure can reduce or eliminate many of these negative impacts. Cities can plant trees that remove particulate matter from the air, absorb traffic noise, and mitigate urban heat island effects (Gómez-Baggethun et al. 2013). More complex and biodiverse vegetation can increase the psychological benefits and sense of well-being people experience when in urban parks (Fuller et al. 2007). Urban greenspace with diverse and complex plantings can also support more wildlife, which provides its own benefits such as pest reduction and pollination (Wratten et al. 2012).

The ability of urban areas to support biodiversity depends on the configuration and quality of greenspaces and their surroundings. Spatial configuration is critical because it defines how well plants and animals can move through the landscape (Aronson et al. 2017). Local vegetation characteristics and the types of management interventions are also important, defining which species are able to use existing greenspaces. Thus, building biodiverse cities will require a combination of large-scale planning and local management actions that work together to achieve the best possible outcomes for biodiversity (Aronson et al. 2017).

Why native biodiversity?

Native plants play an important role in supporting native wildlife (Chapin III et al. 2000). Animals and plants have frequently evolved together, and these deep co-evolutionary relationships often mean that non-native plants do not provide the same resources to animals (Agosta 2006, Strauss et al. 2006, Narango et al. 2018). Native biodiversity is also a significant element of resilience and climate adaptation planning. In California, for example, native oak trees are likely to be good choices for a warmer and less predictable future because of their ability to tolerate both drought and heat (Kueppers et al. 2005, McLaughlin and Zavaleta 2012). Promoting native plants in urban areas can help these landscapes support wildlife populations and is a key component of global conservation for these species. Urban wildlife can also inspire awe and foster a sense of connection to place for urban residents, which can motivate stewardship and investment in conservation (Cox and Gaston 2016).

ABOUT THIS DOCUMENT

Building biodiverse cities will require planning that is based on and informed by the best available science. While the field of urban ecology has grown rapidly, most of its findings remain relatively inaccessible, scattered across thousands of research papers in scientific journals. This report synthesizes a rich body of research to fill this gap, creating accessible and practical guidance for how to apply urban biodiversity science. The result is intended for use by anyone involved in planning for ecosystem health in cities, including government agencies, non-profits, city planners, and landscape architects.

The next chapter identifies seven biodiversity-supporting elements that can be applied across many cities. Chapter 3 is a case study of Silicon Valley, demonstrating how scientific concepts and local data can be applied to urban biodiversity planning. Chapter 4 provides recommendations for creating and implementing a biodiversity plan. Together, these chapters provide a scientific foundation, community context, and example application needed to inform biodiversity planning at any scale.

Valley Oak in Lafayette, CA (Photo courtesy of Erica Spotswood)

Biodiversity in the city: A short history

For three quarters of a century, cities have been considered biological deserts where native plants and animals do not flourish. In 1953, Colin Matheson, the head of the department of Zoology at the National Museum of Wales, published musings lamenting the lack of wildlife in cities, the proliferation of unwanted animal pests, and the disconnection from nature experienced by city-dwellers in Great Britain (Matheson 1953). Ahead of his time, Matheson identified many issues that are now recognized as central challenges to creating cities where nature can thrive.

Less widely recognized is that cities already do support a wide range of plants and animals, often thriving unnoticed in our midst. In addition to ubiquitous urban species, such as rats and pigeons, many native species like coyotes, various songbirds, and peregrine falcons are also found cities across the United States. Yet we know that not all species can survive in cities, and that from the wandering coyote's perspective, not all patches of urban land are created equal. We can learn much about how to support biodiversity in cities by examining which species tend to thrive in them, and what places tend to support the most diverse suites of organisms.

Biodiversity in cities has also changed over time. Across much of the United States, the development of urban centers, followed by suburban expansion after World War II, had profound impacts on the biodiversity of the affected landscapes. Initially, this development led to dramatic declines in native biodiversity and increases in non-native and invasive species. More recently, there has been a rebound in some species (Robinson et al. 1994, Weaver and Garman 1994, Bertin 2002, Er et al. 2005), both in the United States and worldwide (Luniak 2004, Geiger et al. 2018). Many landscapes once cleared for development have been revegetated, and shrubs and trees have matured.

Changing trends in urban planning that place a greater emphasis on tree canopy cover and other green infrastructure have led to focused "greening" efforts (Li et al. 2005).However, despite these trends, most cities lack a coherent strategy for enhancing biodiversity (Nilon et al. 2017), and most urban greening efforts do not focus on achieving ecological benefits. This report is intended to provide guidance on how biodiversity can be incorporated into these activities at a variety of scales, from residential yards to regional planning. Incorporating biodiversity-supporting actions into existing urban greening can help increase the value and resilience of these efforts.

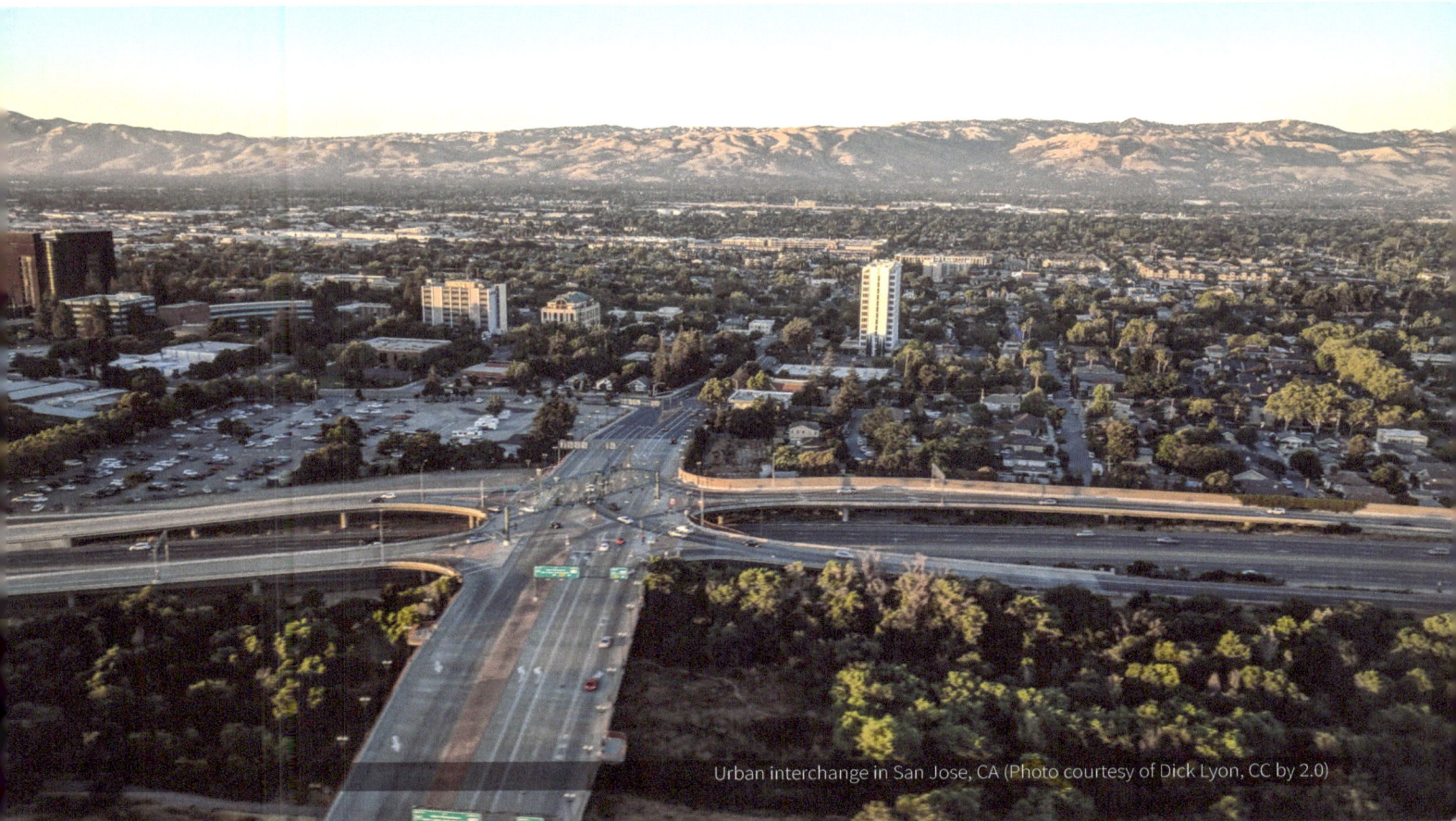

Urban interchange in San Jose, CA (Photo courtesy of Dick Lyon, CC by 2.0)

What about communities?

In this report, we focus on the scientific findings, principles, and analyses that can support urban biodiversity planning rather than the social and community-based steps for developing and implementing a coordinated plan for urban biodiversity. Urban spaces are socially constructed and shaped by both personal preferences and political processes, in which technical information plays a supporting role. Science-based tools like those proposed in this report will be most useful in service of community-driven actions that achieve local priorities. Successful city-scale biodiversity planning will involve partnerships among local community groups, residents, landowners, and public agencies to create a democratic and pluralistic vision that engages non-professionals and leverages local place-based knowledge and priorities.

There are a variety of advantages to this two-way information transfer. Meetings between stakeholder groups are an opportunity for group learning related to biodiversity science. These meetings can also spur urban biodiversity initiatives that are driven by local values and preferences about the landscape, which ultimately shape what kinds and amounts of greenspace local communities will support and take care of. Greater participation by communities may even result in higher potential biodiversity in greenspaces (Dennis and James 2016). However, biodiversity initiatives will also conflict at times with other goals and necessitate trade-offs. An ongoing conversation among stakeholders can both ground biodiversity planning in practical considerations and set the stage for the negotiation of competing interests. For urban biodiversity initiatives to be successful, they will need to provide well-recognized functional and aesthetic benefits that generate a broad base of support.

Existing research can point to some priorities and trade-offs that are likely to impact biodiversity planning efforts, particularly in residential areas. The smaller scale of parcels and number of landowners in these areas pose a challenge to coordinating biodiversity improvements but also an opportunity for aggregate impacts. Urban residents value and benefit from biodiversity in urban greenspaces (Fuller et al. 2007, Schwartz et al. 2014), but biodiversity is usually not the primary factor motivating the management of residential yards or public greenspaces. Rather, ease of maintenance, aesthetic quality, and value for recreation and relaxation are often more important considerations (Larson et al. 2009, Harris et al. 2012). Normative pressures may drive residents to manage yards to achieve standards set by neighbors and cultural expectations, often for neat, well-maintained spaces (Nassauer et al. 2009). Additionally, making changes to yard landscaping requires time and resources that may not be available for many residents. Understanding the importance of these different priorities and potential barriers to the implementation of biodiversity initiatives in a given community is an important step in creating a successful program promoting biodiversity in privately managed urban greenspaces.

Conducting a social assessment can also help identify areas with the most community and political will, where initiatives are likely to be feasible and sustainable. In areas where residential land uses predominate, public participation is key because landowner decisions define the success of biodiversity improvements. In areas with larger parcels zoned for commercial and office use, the greater size and more frequent redesign leads to

Planting in East Palo Alto, CA (Photo courtesy of Canopy)

Green Roof at the California Academy of Sciences (Photo courtesy of SF Planning Department)

opportunities for the creation and expansion of habitat patches and corridors. Regardless of the size or ownership of the spaces involved, most biodiversity activities in cities depend on public support and the willingness of private landowners. Thus aligning biodiversity goals with other priorities is an essential element of success. Public participation can help create the alignment and ongoing engagement necessary for projects to succeed and have an impact.

In many cities, disadvantaged communities face long histories of environmental injustice, and as a result, greenspace access, tree canopy cover, and metrics of biodiversity are often correlated with income and race (Luz de la Maza et al. 2002, Greene et al. 2018, Leong et al. 2018). At the same time, urban greening can provide a variety of benefits to communities, from stress relief to better health, heat island mitigation, and pollution control (Hartig et al. 2014). Evidence for the health benefits of nature is strong and growing, and may be particularly important in lower income communities (Mitchell and Popham 2008, Browning and Rigolon 2018). Given the potential for greenspaces to improve people's quality of life, strategic implementation of biodiversity actions can align with environmental justice goals.

Urban greening interventions also present a paradox in disadvantaged communities. While urban greening can provide a pathway towards redressing environmental injustice, these same actions can increase property values (Escobedo et al. 2011, Li et al. 2015), leading in some cases to displacement and gentrification. In order for underserved communities to reap the benefits of urban greenspaces, it is essential that greening projects are developed alongside programs that minimize the risks of displacement, such as affordable housing construction and rent stabilization. Gentrification is a growing challenge in urban areas irrespective of greening efforts, and in many cities incremental, community-driven greening may not be a major driver of gentrification on its own. However, addressing this risk through coordinating ecological improvements and housing policy is critical to ensuring the benefits of greening are shared equitably.

What about climate change?

Cities are on the frontlines of climate change. Among the many risks, rising sea levels, increased flooding, more frequent droughts and heat waves, and more devastating wildfires are challenging urban infrastructure and can lead to significant economic, environmental, and health impacts (Grimm et al. 2008, Hunt and Watkiss 2011). Because many cities lie along waterways and near coasts, they are vulnerable to rising seas and storm surges, which lead to increased flooding and sometimes a breakdown in key services like wastewater treatment (Major et al. 2011). Urban microclimates are also several degrees warmer than rural landscapes (Tan et al. 2010). Climate change is increasing the magnitude and duration of heat waves and increasing the impact of urban heat islands (Meehl and Tebaldi 2004, Tan et al. 2010). Extreme heat events have significant health consequences for people, exacerbating other conditions among vulnerable populations and even leading to heat-related deaths (Luber and McGeehin 2008).

Mitigating greenhouse gas emissions and adapting to a changing climate must be pursued in tandem, and will require cities to invest in a variety of measures, including energy shifts, infrastructure changes, policy and insurance mechanisms, and green infrastructure (Ürge-Vorsatz et al. 2018). Some adaptation measures, such as building sea walls, may have negative impacts on biodiversity. In contrast, many nature-based approaches to adaptation have the potential to support both biodiversity conservation and climate change mitigation. Tidal marshes can help protect shorelines from rising seas (Duarte et al. 2013), trees can mitigate extreme heat and store carbon (Stone et al. 2009), and green infrastructure can reduce flood risk (Ürge-Vorsatz et al. 2018). Some of these approaches may perform better and cost less than traditional engineered infrastructure (Currin et al. 2017, Smith et al. 2017) while providing other co-benefits such as new recreational opportunities.

Harnessing the full potential of nature-based approaches for climate adaptation will require incorporating biodiversity into early planning stages. Many cities around the world are already creating climate adaptation plans (Hunt and Watkiss 2011), and these plans can incorporate biodiversity goals alongside climate goals. Doing so can help align biodiversity and climate adaptation goals. For example, in California ecosystems, planting native oak trees can support biodiversity, reduce irrigation, store carbon, and provide dense shade (Spotswood et al. 2017). In other cases, prioritizing nature-based solutions for biodiversity may lead to choices to avoid traditional infrastructure, such as seawalls, in favor of green or hybrid options, such as creating marshes, nourished beaches or horizontal levees. These solutions may be preferable if all benefits are assessed holistically.

San Francisco Embarcadero (Photo courtesy of Michelle Ursino, CC by 2.0)

Creating space for nature in cities can also help curb the direct threats that climate change poses to biodiversity. Both contemporary and historical records show species shifting their ranges, adapting through evolutionary change, tolerating new conditions, or modifying behavior while staying in the same place in response to past and present climate shifts (Nogués-Bravo et al. 2018). Traits such as the ability to disperse to new areas and physiological tolerance of warmer temperatures can affect how each species responds. Taken together, this will likely lead to a global reshuffling in the distribution of species, with profound consequences for both ecological communities and human well-being (Pecl et al. 2017). Widespread extinction is also likely and climate change is expected to surpass habitat modification as the primary driver of species loss (Nogués-Bravo et al. 2018).

Landscape patterns such as regional connectivity and the distribution of habitats can influence how species respond to climate change (Lyford et al. 2003, Nogués-Bravo et al. 2018). These patterns influence the ability of plants and animals to disperse to new areas as the climate shifts, and thus affects their ability to successfully track climate change. Given their important role, enhancing regional connectivity and creating and protecting large patches of urban habitat may enable some species to tolerate climate shifts in situ, and will likely assist others as they move to track climate shifts (Rastandeh and Pedersen Zari 2018). The intensive management that is possible in cities can also provide unique opportunities for biodiversity conservation that may help species cope with climate change. This report provides a framework for how to plan for biodiversity conservation in cities. These efforts can help today, and are likely to become even more important as the impacts of climate change accelerate. §

DEFINITIONS

BIODIVERSITY: The variety and abundance of species within a given area. In this report, we focus specifically on native plant and animal species diversity (although genetic, functional, and ecosystem diversity are also important measures) in urban areas.

NATIVE: Plant and animal species that have evolved in a specific geography (including nearby species that may be appropriate in the near future, given anticipated range shifts as the climate changes).

URBAN: An area of high human population and significant built infrastructure. In this report, "urban areas" and "cities" are used interchangeably.

GREENSPACE: An area with grass, trees, or other vegetation primarily dedicated to aesthetic, recreational or habitat preservation purposes in a city.

PATCH: A contiguous patch of greenspace in a city. In this report, we define patches as greenspaces of 2 acres or larger in size (see Chapter 2, Patch Size, for explanation of this threshold).

MATRIX: Urban areas outside of patches and regional corridors. These spaces include residential yards, public and community spaces, commercial and industrial properties, roads and medians, and parking lots.

URBAN GREENING: Actions taken to increase vegetation cover in urban areas. Some examples include street tree planting; stormwater retention basin and green infrastructure installation; park creation, protection, and enhancement; backyard gardening; commercial landscaping; and pollinator plantings.

2

A
FRAMEWORK
FOR
BIODIVERSITY
ENHANCEMENT
IN CITIES

An Introduction to Urban Biodiversity Science

Urban ecology — or the study of ecology in urban environments — began in the mid-20th century with studies documenting the loss of species as landscapes urbanized. Research specific to urban biodiversity has always been a core component of urban ecology, though the emphasis has shifted through time from comparisons of urban and rural areas to methods informed by landscape ecology that relate patterns in biodiversity to patterns on the landscape (Clergeau et al. 1998, Wu 2014). Over the past few decades, the number of research articles documenting the diversity and distribution of plants and animals in cities has grown into the thousands. This work offers a rich repository of information that can inform how we plan for biodiversity in cities and how we might expect biodiversity to respond to changes in the urban landscape.

What has emerged from urban biodiversity research both confirms our intuition and offers new insight. Not surprisingly, for example, pavement limits biodiversity, and greenspaces support more species (McKinney 2008, Beninde et al. 2015). The quality of greenspaces also matters, and diverse native plants tend to better support wildlife than lawns (Pardee and Philpott 2014, Smith and Fellowes 2014, Aronson et al. 2017). Drawing on studies from 75 cities around the world, a recent study has identified the size of patches of greenspace and connectivity corridors as the two most important predictors of biodiversity (Beninde et al. 2015). Resources such as water features and large trees also have outsized effects, drawing and supporting a diverse array of species (Stagoll et al. 2012, Hill et al. 2017). Likewise, the quality of the surrounding urban landscape (the urban matrix) has an influence on biodiversity within patches of greenspace (Goddard et al. 2010, Norton et al. 2016).

Who will benefit from biodiversity improvements?

In this chapter, we draw from this research, conducted around the globe, to identify seven key elements that contribute to biodiversity in cities. These elements include the most important factors to consider when planning for urban biodiversity. Together, they represent an integrated approach to meeting the diverse life history needs of both wildlife and plants. Implementing improvements within each category will require planning and coordination both regionally across a given urban area and locally within habitat patches. Many of these elements are also likely to prove beneficial for supporting species with climate change.

Individual species respond in complex ways to urbanization. Because both wildlife and plants have dramatically different abilities to disperse across the landscape, different species respond very differently to the same spatial pattern of urban greenspace. For example, two adjacent green areas separated by a road may function as a single patch of habitat for a bird, while the same configuration may produce separate populations of smaller, less mobile organisms that rarely interact with one another.

Species-specific characteristics determine how each will respond to urbanization. While some species are highly sensitive to urbanization, others can adapt to and exploit the conditions found in cities (Evans et al. 2011, Bateman and Fleming 2012). The ability to tolerate urbanization relates to the behavioral and life history characteristics of a species. For example, organisms that can fly tend to respond better to urbanization than ground-dwelling organisms (Evans et al. 2011). Habitat and dietary generalists tend to tolerate urbanization better than specialists (Sol et al. 2014, Brown and Graham 2015). In birds, ground-nesting species tend to be highly sensitive to urbanization, whereas species that nest off the ground are often more tolerant (Evans et al. 2011, Sol et al. 2014). Plants with rapid life history strategies, including many commonly recognized as weeds, are often more successful in urban areas (McKinney 2002, Palma et al. 2017). In addition, plants with traits that people prefer, such as shade provision, beautiful flowers, or low maintenance requirements, may be more likely to be introduced and cultivated in urban spaces (Kendal et al. 2012). Species that are more sensitive to urbanization may still be present in urban areas, but restricted to large patches of intact greenspace, such as within urban parks. In contrast, more urban-tolerant species can better use resources in the urbanized matrix between large patches of greenspace, and are therefore more likely to occur across the urban landscape.

Home range size is a particularly important determinant of how animal species respond to urbanization because it is strongly linked to how an organism copes with fragmentation. Species with large home ranges, such as large mammals and some birds, require large areas to survive. For these species to persist in urban areas, they will need to use the matrix around patches of greenspace. In contrast, species with small home ranges may be able to survive in small patches of greenspace even if they are unable to tolerate

Bobcat in Santa Teresa County Park, California (Photo courtesy of Don Debold, CC-by 2.0)

urbanization. However, short dispersal distances may isolate populations of these species and increase the likelihood of their extinction. Highly sensitive animals with large home ranges may still be able to pass through the urban landscape if high-quality corridors are present. Similarly, plants with different dispersal and reproduction strategies may be more or less sensitive to patch size and conditions in the surrounding matrix, and may or may not be able to disperse through unsuitable areas of the landscape.

Specific habitat requirements can also dictate whether a species can persist in a given patch. Organisms with strong links to particular host plants or pollinators, for example, may be excluded from patches of greenspace that lack the associated species. Some species require multiple adjacent habitats during different stages of life, such as amphibians that require aquatic habitat connected to uplands for reproduction and foraging. Because responses to urbanization are highly species-specific, no single intervention can support all species. Some, for example, will respond most strongly to large patches of greenspace, whereas others will respond most to the addition of particular features such as water or large trees. It is therefore the integration of all the elements together that has the greatest chance of supporting the largest number of species.

In the following pages, we introduce and define seven elements of biodiversity support. These elements are synthesized from a wide range of urban biodiversity research. Some of the key papers we used in developing these elements can be found in Appendix A. We provide the scientific support and background for the elements, as well as specific recommendations for how each can be implemented. Future chapters use Silicon Valley as a case study to apply these elements (Chapter 3), and provide guidance on how to develop a biodiversity plan that draws on the science of urban biodiversity (Chapter 4).

ELEMENTS THAT SUPPORT URBAN BIODIVERSITY

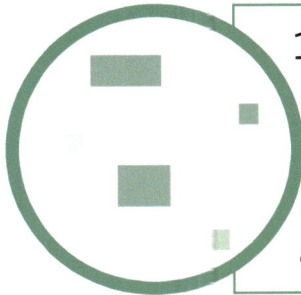

1 · PATCH SIZE

The size of a contiguous patch of greenspace in a city. We define patches as contiguous greenspaces of at least 2 acres in size.

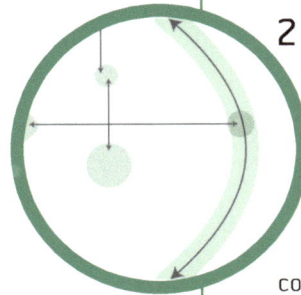

2 · CONNECTIONS

Features in the urban landscape that facilitate the movement of plants and animals. Connections include corridors (thin stretches of greenspace that promote linear movement) and stepping stones (sets of discrete but nearby patches that together promote connectivity across the landscape).

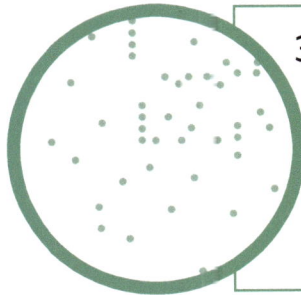

3 · MATRIX QUALITY

Habitat elements that support ecological process and movement in the urban matrix between patches of greenspace and corridors.

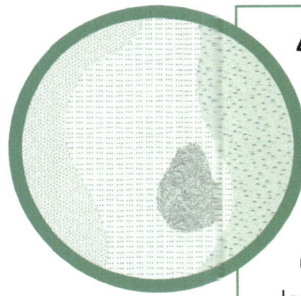

4 · HABITAT DIVERSITY

The type, number, and spatial distribution of habitat types within an urban area. Together, mosaics of habitats create diversity in habitat types at the landscape scale.

5 · NATIVE PLANT VEGETATION

Plant species long evolved in a specific geography (including nearby species that may be appropriate in the near future, given anticipated range shifts with climate change).

6 · SPECIAL RESOURCES

Unique habitat features necessary to support species' life history requirements, including large trees, wetlands, streams, and rivers.

7 · MANAGEMENT

Human activities and planning that promote positive biodiversity outcomes.

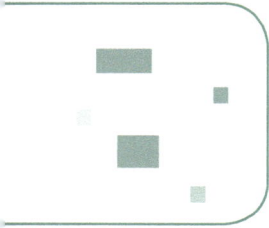

PATCH SIZE

DEFINITION

The size of a contiguous patch of greenspace in a city. We define patches here as greenspaces of at least 2 acres in size.

Significance in urban areas

In a recent analysis summarizing patterns of biodiversity from 75 cities worldwide, researchers identified patch size as one of two most important drivers of how much biodiversity is found in urban greenspaces (Beninde et al. 2015). This finding is consistent with research outside cities: one of the most predictable patterns in ecology is the relationship between the size of a patch and the number of species found within it (Connor and McCoy 1979).

Larger patches support more species for two reasons. First, large patches tend to have more types of microhabitats, creating more variation that broadens the number of species that can find adequate resources. Second, large patches can support higher numbers of individuals of each species because they contain more total resources. Larger populations buffer against population crashes and local extinction, enabling larger patches to support more total numbers of species. Similarly-sized patches can also support more biodiversity if, in addition to being large, they are less isolated

(Nielsen et al. 2014), have less edge compared to core area (e.g., Soga et al. 2014), and if the overall habitat quality is higher (Angold et al. 2006).

Knowing that patch size matters in cities leads to two practical questions. First, how big does a greenspace need to be to be considered a 'patch', and second, what size patch is 'big enough' to support biodiversity? While these questions have no firmly established scientific answers, several studies have used the relationship between the size of a patch and the number of species it supports to identify thresholds below which species richness begins to rapidly decline (e.g., Drinnan 2005, Arca et al. 2012). A recent summary of this work (Beninde et al. 2015) found that a common threshold for defining a 'patch' was 1 ha (2.4 acres). Similarly, the average patch size below which biodiversity rapidly declined was 4.4 ha (10.9 acres). Based on this work, we recommend that greenspaces should be at least 2 acres to be considered a patch, and at least 10 acres to support significant biodiversity. These patches of greater than 10 acres will likely act as local hubs of biodiversity support. However, many species that depend on large contiguous habitats will be restricted to much larger patches.

Cities often contain only a small number of large patches of greenspace (usually large parks). Large parks can support many species, often acting as regional hubs of biodiversity (Beninde et al. 2015). Large patches can also help sustain species that use both the patch and the surrounding urbanized matrix, reinforcing the ability of the matrix to support biodiversity (Whited et al. 2000, Björklund et al. 2010). Some species are highly area-sensitive or intolerant of urbanization and will only be found in large patches of continuous habitat where edges are minimized (Blair 1996, Beninde et al. 2015). Some migratory species also use large parks as stopover habitat during long migrations (Craves 2009, Matthews and Rodewald 2010, Seewagen et al. 2010). Several studies have quantified the size of patch that is too small to support area-sensitive or forest-interior species. These results are summarized by Bendinde and co-authors (Beninde et al. 2015), who found that the average patch size necessary to support area-sensitive or forest-interior species is 53.3 ha (132 acres). We suggest that patches of 130 acres or larger should be considered regional biodiversity hubs, of special significance city-wide for supporting unique suites of species.

MIGRATING SONGBIRD STOPOVERS

During migration, songbirds seek patches of habitat where they can rest and refuel. After days of flying, birds arrive exhausted, having lost large amounts of body weight. They spend several days recovering at stopover sites, regaining body weight and preparing for the next leg of their long journey. The role of good stopover habitat along migration routes is therefore critical to the survival of birds that migrate long distances.

Three large parks in New York City (including Prospect Park, a highly isolated park of ~526 acres in Brooklyn), lie at the nexus of four major bird migration routes used by over 100 species of songbirds. During migration season, exceptional concentrations of migrants can be found in these parks. A recent investigation of Swainson's thrushes (*Catharus ustulatus*), ovenbirds (*Seiurus aurocapilla*), and yellow-rumped warblers (*Setophaga coronata*) found these birds were more densely concentrated in urban parks than in adjacent open spaces outside the city. Despite the large difference in bird density, all three species were found to refuel and gain body weight similarly in the urban and rural sites after several days of rest (Seewagen et al. 2010).

Swainson's Thrush *(Catharus ustulatus)* (Photo courtesy of Melissa McMasters, CC by 2.0)

Who benefits from large patches?

Area-sensitive species that require large patches of habitat and urban-sensitive wildlife may be the biggest beneficiaries of large patches. In some cases, these species may be restricted to regional biodiversity hubs. Larger patches can also support more substantial populations of plants, and these spaces may serve an important conservation function for species that are threatened or rare.

Supporting area-sensitive wildlife in urban areas requires considering their life history and habitat needs. For example, a single patch may be sufficient to support a family group, pair, or colony of a highly mobile species if these individuals are connected to other members of their species in adjacent patches. On the other hand, the urban matrix may isolate populations of small, ground-dwelling, or area-sensitive species. In these cases, patch sizes may need to be large enough to support a self-sustaining population.

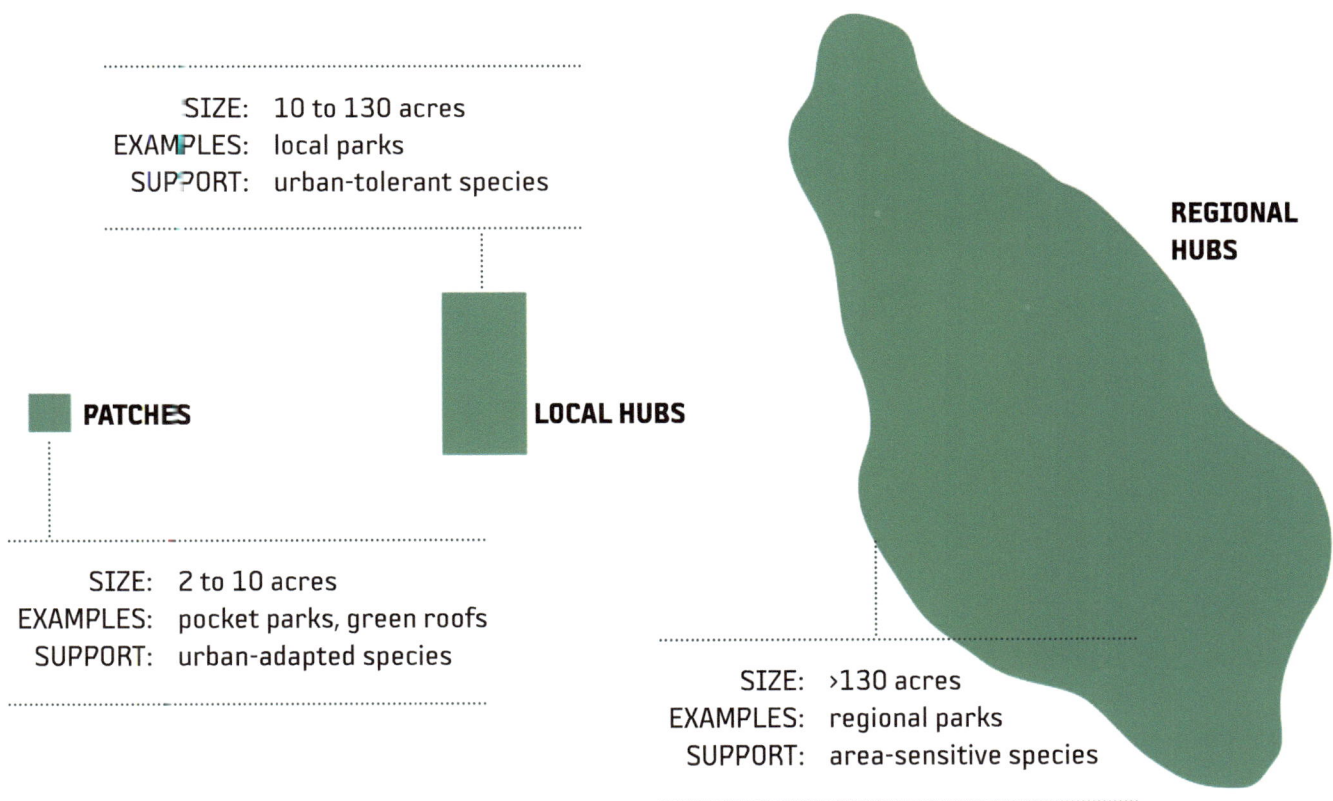

SIZE: 10 to 130 acres
EXAMPLES: local parks
SUPPORT: urban-tolerant species

PATCHES

LOCAL HUBS

REGIONAL HUBS

SIZE: 2 to 10 acres
EXAMPLES: pocket parks, green roofs
SUPPORT: urban-adapted species

SIZE: >130 acres
EXAMPLES: regional parks
SUPPORT: area-sensitive species

Bosque de Chapultepec in Mexico City, Mexico (Photo courtesy of Ricardo Gomez Garrido, CC by 2.0)

Guidelines

1. Prioritize the creation and protection of regional biodiversity hubs. Ongoing protection and enhancement of habitat quality in existing regionally-significant patches is essential for supporting city-wide biodiversity. Creating new large patches, particularly in cities that have few or no large parks, can also be made a priority during biodiversity planning.

2. Prioritize the protection of large remnants of high-quality habitat. Patches that already contain high-quality habitat can (and may already) support more biodiversity than patches of equivalent size that have been highly modified. Patches with high-quality habitat should require less investment to achieve biodiversity objectives, and will require less active restoration to recover ecological functions.

3. Expand existing patches. When planning future acquisitions, consider possibilities to expand existing large, high-quality patches. This can be an effective strategy for maximizing biodiversity, and can help to create local or regional hubs of biodiversity by building on existing greenspace resources.

4. Reduce edges. Square or circular patches have more core habitat and shorter perimeters, and are thus more suitable to area-sensitive species than long, skinny patches of similar size.

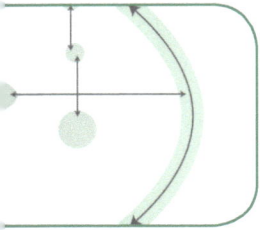

ELEMENT 02:
CONNECTIONS

DEFINITION

Features in the urban land-scape that facilitate the move-ment of plants and animals. Connections include corridors (thin stretches of greenspace that promote linear move-ment) and stepping stones (sets of discrete but nearby patches that together pro-mote connectivity across the landscape).

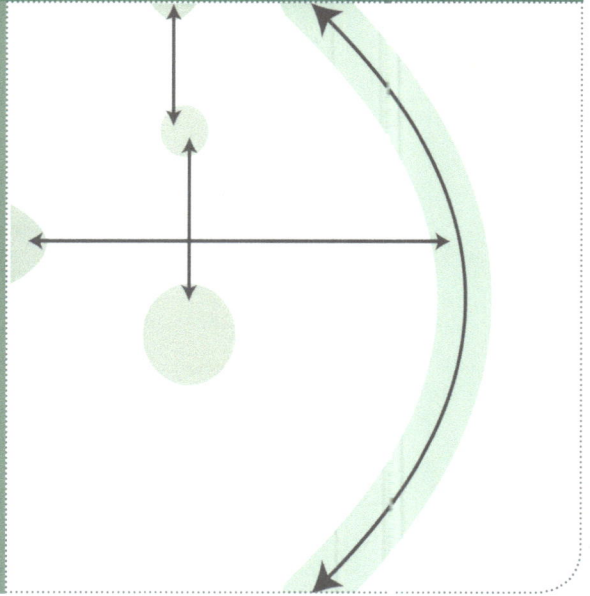

Significance in urban areas

Connectivity across the landscape is one of the most important elements driving biodiversity in cities (Beninde et al. 2015). Landscapes with high connectivity may provide for higher numbers of species (Gledhill et al. 2008, Shanahan et al. 2011), including those that rely strongly on connections in order to tolerate urbanization (Matsuba et al. 2016). The urban environment either supports or inhibits the movement of organisms across the landscape depending on the configuration of patches, corridors, and barriers. Landscapes with many connections and few barriers allow organisms to move freely to access resources, promoting gene flow and allowing organisms to access a variety of habitats during different life stages.

Landscape connections can link habitats and populations to one another, allow movement among different habitat types, and connect terrestrial and aquatic resources. Connections can act as conduits for species to adapt to climate change and migrate after disturbances, and they can facilitate landscape-level ecosystem processes such as nutrient cycling (Thrush et al. 2008, Standish et al. 2013). Hydrological connectivity enables movement in aquatic species, and connectivity among different habitat types can enable species to use different types of habitat across seasons or during different life stages. Connectivity between patches can also directly increase cumulative patch size (Tewksbury et al. 2002).

Physical features that influence connectivity include corridors, stepping stones, and barriers. Corridors are continuous bands of protected vegetation (including riparian areas along streams, or greenways) and are the best way of enhancing connectivity (Beninde et al. 2015). Corridors are most effective if they are both wide and continuous. Large gaps or narrow sections can both reduce the ability of corridors to enhance connectivity (Miltner et al. 2004, Tremblay & St. Claire 2009).

Corridors can facilitate movement within a city (Munshi-South and Kharchenko 2010) and can connect fragmented habitats to large regional biodiversity hubs outside of cities (Gilbert-Norton et al. 2010). Regional corridors that cross an entire city can provide unique opportunities for urban-sensitive species, enabling wide-ranging species to move from open spaces on one side of the city to those on the other. We suggest that these regional corridors, often few in number, have unique significance to biodiversity. Shorter corridors that connect greenspaces to one another can enhance connectivity within the urban landscape. These sources of connectivity can promote local movement and dispersal. Stepping stones, or patches of habitat between large patches or corridors, can enhance connectivity by facilitating movement between them, provided barriers do not interrupt movement (e.g. Zipperer et al. 2012).

Barriers are physical features that reduce connectivity by impeding the movement of organisms, increasing landscape fragmentation and limiting the connectivity of populations (Riley et al. 2006, Tremblay and St. Clair 2011). Common examples in urban areas include roads, parking lots and other impervious surfaces (Rondinini and Doncaster 2002), buildings (Beninde et al. 2016), culverted stream reaches, fencing, and gaps in tree canopy cover (Tremblay and St. Clair 2011, Favaro and Moore 2015). Because vehicles kill animals, and their noise indirectly causes avoidance behavior, roads pose particularly strong barriers for wildlife (Forman 2016). Impervious surfaces and buildings can also act as barriers for organisms that are unable to move around or across them. For plants that depend on animal dispersal, barriers to animals that disperse seeds can also impact connectivity for plants.

Who benefits from connections?

While regional corridors may benefit many species, they can be particularly important for large, wide-ranging animals that are relatively intolerant of urbanization. These species often require continuous, relatively intact habitat for movement through urban areas and may benefit from regional corridors if they permit movement between open spaces on either side of the city (Beier 1995, Tigas et al. 2002, Van Rossum and Triest 2012).

Connectivity between adjacent habitat types can also be beneficial for species that move between habitat types at different times of day, across different seasons, or during different life stages. For example, amphibians require connectivity between terrestrial and aquatic habitat to complete reproduction. Similarly, many species move between different habitat types when going from foraging to roosting. Hydrological connectivity, including connectivity of stream corridors, and connections between riparian and adjacent floodplain habitat can also benefit many aquatic species.

Smaller scale corridors can also support species that do not disperse long distances. For example, enhancing connectivity between adjacent gardens can benefit flying insects (Vergnes et al. 2012). Stepping stones may benefit fewer species than corridors because species that are unable to cross through the urbanized matrix between patches may not use them (e.g., ground-dwelling or other highly urban-sensitive species). Improving connectivity by reducing barriers can reduce mortality in species that are frequently killed by cars or other hazards.

Ohlone Greenway in Berkeley, California (Photo courtesy of Kelzuen, CC by 2.0)

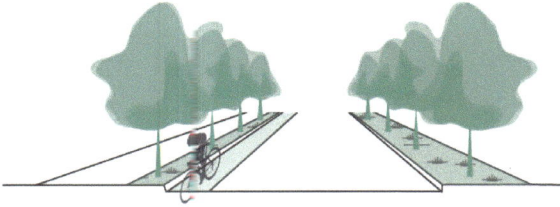

GREEN STREETS

LEVEL: Local Corridor
FUNCTION: Promote local movements and connect patches or larger corridors

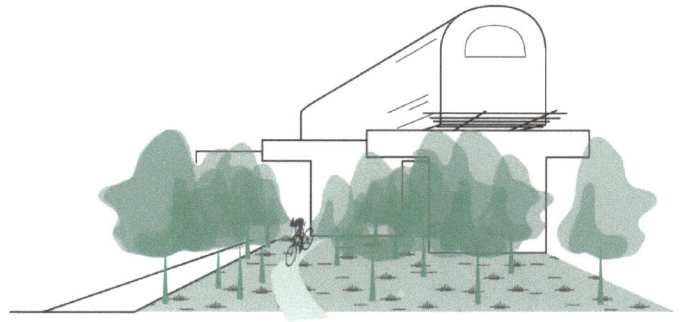

GREENWAYS

LEVEL: Local Corridor
FUNCTION: Promote local movements and connect patches or larger corridors

RIPARIAN CORRIDORS

LEVEL: Regional Corridor
FUNCTION: Promote regional movement across cities

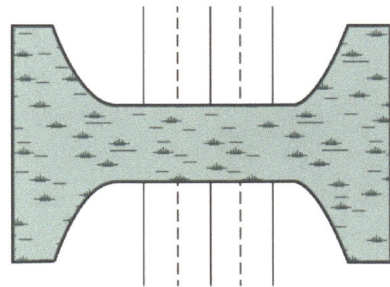

WILDLIFE CROSSINGS

LEVEL: Barrier Reducer
FUNCTION: Reduce road-related mortality

Guidelines

1. Prioritize the creation and protection of regional corridors.
Where regional corridors already exist, improvements can be made through active restoration to improve habitat quality and increase width. Where they do not yet exist, acquiring greenspace to link patches together can build towards the development of regional corridors.

2. Fill gaps in corridors. Gaps in corridors can be filled where breaks in the continuity of vegetation are created by urbanization or where barriers are created by roads or other physical features. Priority should be placed on actions that can fill gaps, such as strategic acquisition of land.

3. Reduce barriers. Activities that reduce barriers caused by roads, impervious surfaces, fences, and buildings include mitigating sensitive road crossings with underpasses or overpasses, daylighting streams, and removing fencing.

4. Protect, acquire, and improve stepping stones. New stepping stones can enhance connectivity between large, high-quality patches. City parks, networks of connected backyards, and flood detention basins are all examples of urban greening actions that can create stepping stones.

5. Prioritize hydrological connectivity and connections between different habitat types. Connecting adjacent habitats can be achieved by acquiring, protecting, and improving habitat patches in strategic locations (e.g. upland patches adjacent to corridors of riparian habitat). Hydrological connectivity can be improved by removing barriers to fish passage, or by setting back or removing levees to reconnect streams to floodplains.

6. Improve within-patch connectivity. Connectivity within greenspaces can be enhanced by creating high-quality habitat around existing features such as water features or large trees. Reducing or removing local barriers, such as through road removal or seasonal closure of roads during peak ecological activity, can also serve to enhance connectivity within greenspaces.

Charleston Retention Basin in Mountain View, California (Photo courtesy of Shira Bezalel)

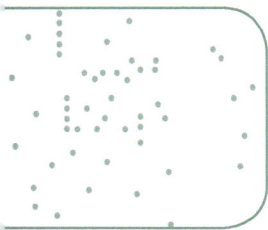

ELEMENT 03:
MATRIX QUALITY

DEFINITION
Habitat elements that support ecological process and movement in the urban matrix between patches of greenspace and corridors.

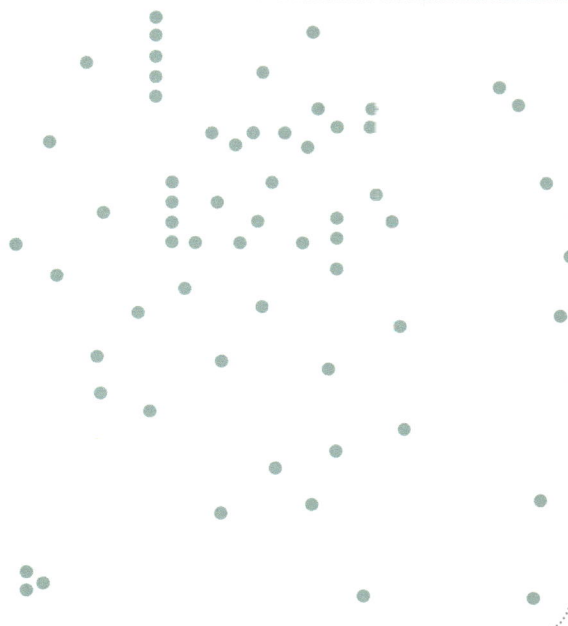

Significance in urban areas

The capacity of patches of greenspace in cities to support biodiversity depends in part on the habitat quality of the adjacent urban area. Patches of similar size amidst high-quality habitat in the urban matrix tend to support more species than those with surrounding high impervious cover and low habitat quality (Goddard et al. 2010, Ikin et al. 2013, Norton et al. 2016). Improving matrix quality can have a number of benefits for biodiversity. For example, high matrix quality around existing patches of greenspace can increase the effective size of a patch, allowing plants and animals additional space for life functions and movement.

Improving the quality of the matrix can enable patches to support more species (Ikin et al. 2013) and higher numbers of individuals of each species (Loeb et al. 2009), buffering populations from local extinction (Williams et al. 2009). Matrix habitat can also increase connectivity by enabling organisms to move through the matrix from one patch to another (Malanson 2003, Baum et al. 2004, Evans et al. 2017). Low-quality matrix can impede movement (ex. Evans et al. 2017) and the effectiveness of corridors and stepping stones can depend strongly on the surrounding matrix (Baum et al. 2004, see related element Connections). Higher matrix quality is also linked to better support of populations and richness of species in the matrix itself (Fernandez-Juricic 2000, Goddard et al. 2010, Belaire et al. 2014, Greco and Airola 2018). Improving matrix quality may also reduce edge effects, or the negative effects of fragmentation associated with the boundary between patches of habitat and adjacent urban land (Driscoll et al. 2013).

Matrix quality can be improved through a variety of urban greening interventions. Adding trees and other vegetation along streets and in private yards can provide cover and food sources for wildlife and increase the diversity of plants supported in the urban landscape (Bateman and Fleming 2012). Higher proportions of greenspace and tree canopy (Ziter 2016), and increased native plant abundance and richness (see element Native Vegetation) have all been found to improve animal biodiversity both in the matrix and in adjacent patches of greenspaces. Matrix quality can also be improved by increasing vegetation complexity by adding shrubs to create vertical structure (Fernandez-Juricic 2000, Belaire et al. 2014). Improving available soil and soil health can also increase the ability of native plants to establish and thrive (Pickett et al. 2011). Finally, preserving large trees, water features, and other special resources can enhance the quality of matrix habitat (see element Special Resources).

Opportunities to improve matrix quality depend on patterns of land use and land cover. Urban density and the footprint of individual buildings can impact the amount of space available for plant growth (Cadenasso et al. 2007). Building height and infrastructure constraints can also potentially impact tree canopy cover. Planning with these considerations in mind can help make for more effective matrix quality improvements.

Who benefits from matrix quality improvements?

Habitat and diet generalists and aerial species may benefit most from improving matrix quality because they are more likely to tolerate urbanization, and are more able to use multiple adjacent resources as they move through landscape (Goddard et al. 2010). For example, flying animals such as birds and winged insects can more easily traverse barriers such as roads. Native plant species that are planted by people can also themselves benefit from matrix improvements. For example, plants that are aesthetically pleasing or valued by people may be planted more frequently, and allowed to persist more often than species perceived to be weedy.

MATRIX ELEMENTS:

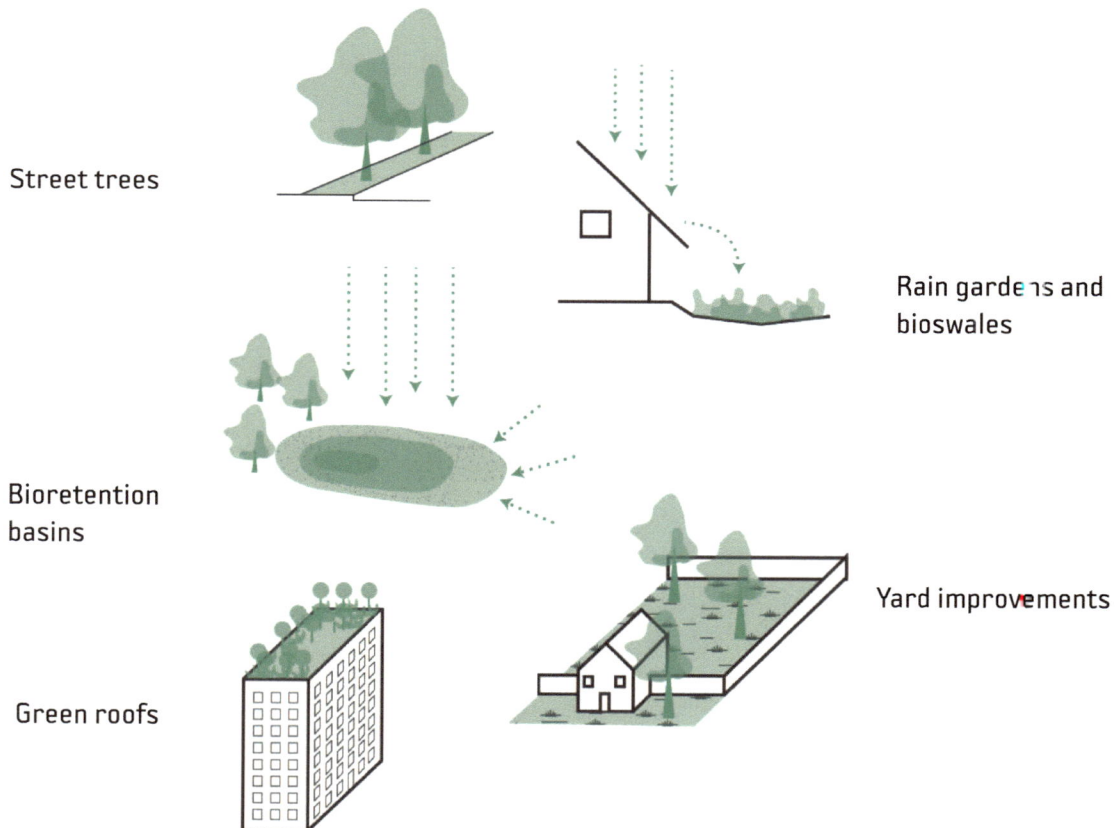

Street trees

Rain gardens and bioswales

Bioretention basins

Yard improvements

Green roofs

Anna's Hummingbird *(Calypte anna)* (Photo courtesy of Shira Bezalel)

COORDINATED MATRIX IMPROVEMENTS:

Between patches can increase patch connectivity

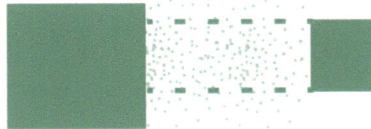

Around patches can increase the effective size of patches

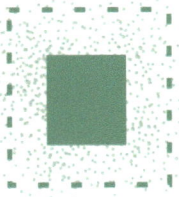

Grouped between patches can create habitat complexes that act as stepping stones

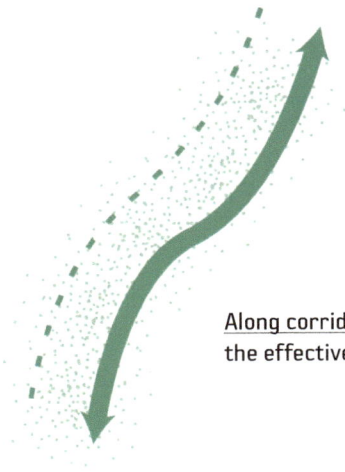

Along corridors can increase the effective width of corridors

Legend

Matrix Elements

Patches

Corridors

Guidelines

1. Prioritize matrix improvements around existing patches. Improving food resources and cover around patches can effectively increase the size of the patch. Some of the most valuable matrix improvements may be those that increase the effective patch size of biodiversity hubs, or other large patches of high-quality habitat (see Patch Size), though matrix improvements around smaller patches can also be beneficial.

2. Prioritize matrix improvements where they will enhance connectivity. Matrix improvements such as increasing tree canopy cover or planting the appropriate native vegetation to fill gaps in regional corridors may be the most effective action to increase landscape connectivity, though new connections between patches of habitat are also important.

3. Create habitat complexes in the urban matrix. Matrix quality can be improved in areas that are not adjacent to regional corridors or patches of greenspace by coordinating actions to form habitat complexes that function like small patches. These habitat complexes can create stepping stones between patches and can support biodiversity in their own right. One approach is to center the creation of habitat complexes around existing special resources such as large trees or water features. For example, in California, planting native oaks around existing large oaks may enable support for acorn woodpecker colonies and other oak-associated species in the urban landscape (Spotswood et al. 2017).

(Photo courtesy of Robin Grossinger)

Hauser & Wirth in Los Angeles, California (Photo courtesy of Robin Grossinger)

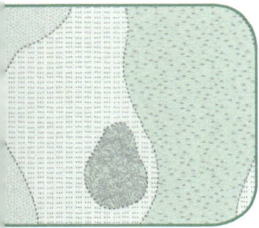

ELEMENT 04:
HABITAT DIVERSITY

DEFINITION
The type, number, and spatial distribution of habitat types within the urban area. Together, mosaics of habitats create diversity in habitat types at the landscape scale.

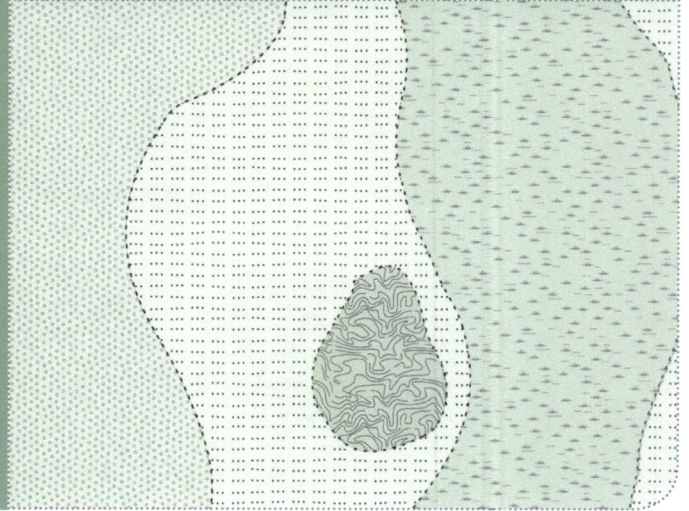

Significance in urban areas

Habitats are made up of assemblages of plants and animals that live together in similar types of locations. In relatively undisturbed areas, landscapes are usually characterized by mosaics of habitat types that follow physical and environmental gradients. This diversity is critical for supporting overall biodiversity (Tews et al. 2004). Landscapes with more habitat diversity can support higher numbers of species because they contain more total resources and niches for a diverse array of organisms to fill (Tews et al. 2004). Additionally, habitat diversity enables species to access resources in multiple types of habitats as they move across the landscape (Tscharntke et al. 2012). Thus, it is both the diversity of habitats and their spatial arrangement that fosters biodiversity (Tscharntke et al. 2012).

Urbanization leads to fragmentation, which can disconnect formerly adjacent habitat types. Widespread planting of common non-native plants exacerbates fragmentation by homogenizing vegetation and reducing the potential for multiple distinct habitat types to be expressed across urban landscapes (McKinney 2006, Schwartz et al. 2006). The impact of habitat diversity on biodiversity has not been well studied in cities, presumably due to the difficulty in establishing appropriate study designs, given the fragmentation and homogenization that has already occurred. Nevertheless, there is good reason to believe that habitat diversity is as important in urban landscapes as it is in non-urban systems, and the best available supporting evidence comes from studies of urban parks and open spaces.

A number of studies have found that parks with higher habitat diversity support more species (Faeth et al. 2011, Nielsen et al. 2014). Similarly, several studies have found that parks that contain rare and unique remnant habitat types also tend to support distinct assemblages of species specialized to those habitat types. For example, remnant woodlots have higher butterfly and ground beetle diversity than landscaped parks in Tokyo (Soga et al. 2014). Open spaces with rare fynbos shrub land in Cape Town, South Africa support higher bird diversity than areas dominated by an invasive Acacia tree (Dures and Cumming 2010). In San Diego, California, canyons with larger patches of relatively undisturbed chaparral support more chaparral-associated bird species (Soule et al. 1988).

Within habitats, the spatial and vertical arrangement of plants, accompanying physical features, and interactions among plants and animals work together to support biodiversity. Thus, it is not simply the list of plants that occur, but rather how they interact with the physical environment, and the presence of other plants and wildlife that work together to make coherent habitat types. These fine-scale features are important in both urban and non-urban ecosystems. For example, in urban areas the spatial arrangement and diversity of vegetation, the presence of woody debris and leaf litter, and the presence of a multi-layered canopy are all associated with higher biodiversity (Goddard et al. 2010, Shwartz et al. 2013, Le Roux et al. 2014, Beninde et al. 2015, Goddard et al. 2017). It is important to note that the spatial complexity and physical features that define habitats are all highly specific to individual habitat types. Therefore, establishing habitats within an urban landscape should aim to replicate the spatial and physical elements that define each type independently. Doing so requires considering the spatial complexity of plants and the distribution of other "keystone structures", such as trees in a savanna landscape (Tews et al. 2004).

To address the homogenization and lack of habitat diversity in urban landscapes, some scientists have recommended creating habitat zones to guide planting at the city scale. These zones could use historical ecology information as a guide, alongside relevant contemporary information and climate change predictions (Löfvenhaft et al. 2002, Beller et al. 2010). Creating habitat zones could increase the diversity of habitats at the city scale, while also enabling coherence within habitat types (Goddard et al. 2010, Aronson et al. 2017).

Who benefits from habitat type and structure?

Creating a diversity of habitat types across urban landscapes will most benefit native species that can tolerate urbanization. Building a diverse portfolio of habitat types, including rare habitats, will create resources for a broader array of species, including species that are highly specialized to a particular habitat type. Species that use multiple habitats may benefit from habitat adjacency that enables movement across the landscape.

Zone A

Zone B

LEVEL: site scale
BENEFITS: provides habitat
           heterogeneity and
           structure

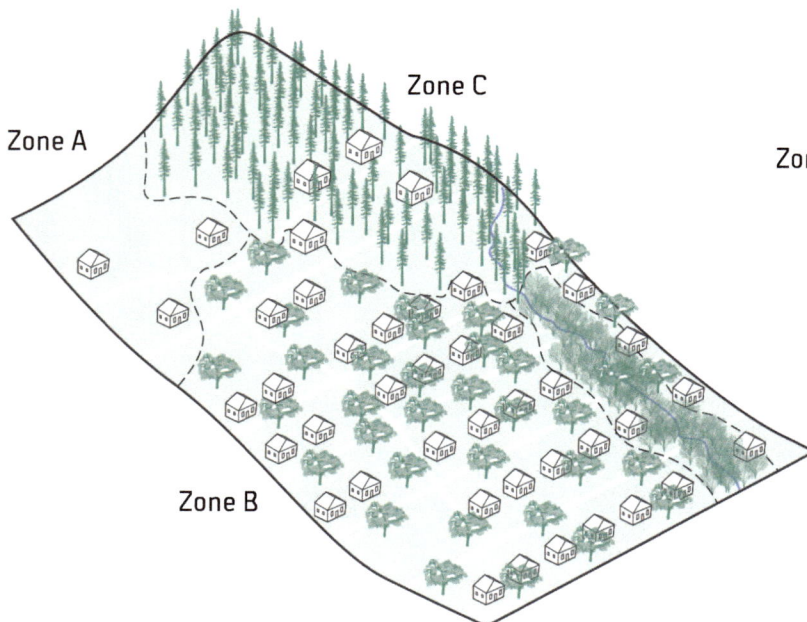

Zone C

Zone A

Zone C

Zone B

LEVEL: landscape scale
BENEFITS: coherence and
           heterogeneity at the
           landscape scale

Guidelines

1. Create habitat zones. Habitat zones based on historical and physical information can be incorporated into a variety of urban greening actions across a variety of land use types, through actions like backyard gardening, street tree programs, landscaping, and park management.

2. Mimic the characteristics of particular habitat types. Urban biodiversity interventions should seek to mimic, recreate, and preserve the spatial and vertical complexity that is characteristic of a particular habitat type.

3. Promote adjacency and connections across habitat types. Creating connections between habitat types can be achieved through matrix improvements and vegetation management within greenspaces. For example, coordinated efforts in residential yards can create more coherent transitions between riparian and upland habitats.

4. Restore and conserve rare habitat types. Patches of remnant and rare habitat types that are uncommon in surrounding landscapes (e.g. sand dunes in San Francisco, CA and montane fynbos in Cape Town, South Africa) deserve special protection and recognition. Protecting remaining tracts of these habitats and restoring them where they historically existed will benefit the plants and animals that rely on the unique resources they provide.

Charleston Retention Basin (Photo courtesy of Shira Bezalel)

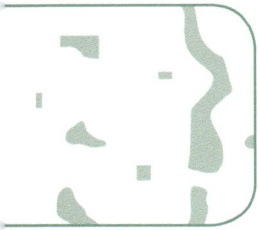

NATIVE VEGETATION

DEFINITION
Plant species long evolved in a specific geography (including anticipated range shifts as the climate changes).

Significance in urban areas

Native plant communities structure and define habitat types, and are critical for supporting a diversity of wildlife. Many studies have found greater biodiversity in urban greenspaces with greater abundance and richness of native plants (Goddard et al. 2010, Aronson et al. 2017, Threlfall et al. 2017). Native plants have complex and interdependent relationships with other organisms, developed through deep shared evolutionary histories (e.g. Ehrlich and Raven 1964). Many insects have strongly specialized relationships with host plants or specialized diets resulting from adaptations to tolerate plant chemical defenses (e.g. high tannin content in oak leaves, Stone et al. 2009). The presence of specialized insects can form the basis of food webs that cascade upwards, enhancing biodiversity of other wildlife. As a result, non-native plants are often poor substitutes for native plants, and exotic-dominated urban habitats tend to support less native wildlife (Goddard et al. 2010, Aronson et al. 2017).

Native plant species can also create favorable soil conditions that facilitate nutrient cycling, regulate the pH and other chemical properties (Dahlgren et al. 1997), and enable interdependent relationships among microbial communities (Dahlgren et al. 2003) and other plants (Brooker et al. 2008). These relationships are often eliminated during development (Carreiro et al. 1999), and can be disrupted by exotic species that change soil properties (e.g. Eucalyptus in Wolf and DiTomaso 2016; garlic mustard in Wolfe et al. 2008). While biodiversity generally increases with greenspace area (see Patch Size), lawns and exotic-dominated plantings can reduce capacity for greenspaces to support biodiversity (Tonietto et al. 2011, Threlfall et al. 2017). Native plants can be integrated into the landscape in underutilized areas of parks and yards without compromising lawns used for recreation.

Remnant patch of native Oaks in Flood Park, Menlo Park, CA (Photo courtesy of Erica Spotswood)

NATIVE SPECIES AND CLIMATE CHANGE

Climate change poses a challenge to native plants and animals [Thomas and Gill 2017]. Individual species will respond differently, and in potentially unpredictable ways. Some will tolerate the new conditions, while others will adapt. Still others will migrate to track a changing climate, and some may go extinct [Feeley et al. 2012]. Providing the maximum support possible to biodiversity is one strategy for helping species cope as climate change accelerates. This support should include a variety of tools, including providing habitat and connectivity where species are today [Heller and Zavaleta 2009].

Cynipid wasp gall in oak tree (Photo courtesy of Jennifer Natali)

Prioritizing native species support within their contemporary ranges is likely to be critical for enabling species to stay in place, adapt, or migrate with climate change. However, even with conservation planning, many native species are likely to be threatened with extinction. For these species, other options, including translocating individuals, either within their existing ranges (e.g., assisted gene flow), or to the leading edge of their ranges where the climate is newly suitable (e.g., assisted migration or assisted colonization) may make sense alongside other conservation measures.

In addition, it may also be necessary to import species from other locations. Preparing now for success in the future is most relevant and pressing for long-lived tree species that will need to tolerate conditions well into the future. Planting trees now to prepare for climate change may be particularly important in cities, where trees are crucial to helping cities adapt (Brandt et al. 2016). Where there is a risk of species loss as the climate shifts, assisted colonization can help replace species and the biological interactions they bring with them (Gallagher et al. 2015). Climate and ecological science can be used to help identify species that may benefit from translocation, and may be able to fill in for missing species in the future (Gallagher et al. 2015). In many cases, this may mean selecting species from nearby regions further south or at lower elevations that are similar to those at risk (Brandt et al. 2016). Species from nearby may be more likely to need translocation, and more likely to already possess the ability to support wildlife.

Both assisted migration and assisted gene flow pose risks, and there are significant unknowns in how species will respond. Among the risks are the potential for translocated species to become invasive, alter species interactions, or introduce novel diseases, all of which could destabilize ecosystems (e.g., Hunter 2007, McLachlan et al. 2007, Aitken and Whitlock 2013). Because species are expected to respond differently to climate change based on a variety of traits, including dispersal ability, physiological tolerance, and genetic diversity, it will be necessary to weigh the risks of translocation against the risk of extinction on a species-by-species basis (Pecl et al. 2017). A recently developed framework for adapting urban forests under climate change suggests using vulnerability assessments across species to combine scientific information with social and organizational information to develop strategies for protecting urban forests under climate change (Brandt et al. 2016). This type of framework may help guide decisions related to appropriate tree choices for the future.

Who benefits from native vegetation?

While many native species can benefit from increased cover and distribution of native plants, wildlife with specialized relationships with individual plant species will benefit in particular. Monarch butterflies (*Danaus plexipus*), for instance, lay their eggs only on milkweeds (*Asclepias* spp. , Sears et al. 2001), and many other insects are dependent on specific native species for food, shelter and reproduction. Species that occupy lost or rare habitats may also benefit. Some examples include neotropical migrants that favor willow groves during migration (Sedgwick 2000), *Cynipid* wasps that specialize on oaks (Cornell 1985), and migrating songbirds that spend part of the year in valley oaks in Sacramentc (Greco and Airola 2018).

Native plants themselves can also benefit from protection and support in cities, particularly for species that face conservation challenges outside urban areas. For example, many native wildflowers face severe competition with non-native annual grasses in grasslands throughout California (D'Antonio et al. 2007). The potential for more intensive management of native wildflowers in gardens and other greenspaces could help to create thriving populations of some species in cities, serving broader conservation goals.

REMOVE INVASIVE SPECIES

PROTECT NATIVE SPECIES

Diversity and abundance

Flowers, fruits, and nuts

365

Year-round resources for wildlife

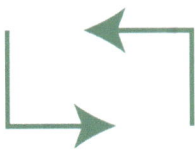

Complementary plants

Guidelines

1. Plant and protect native plants to increase patch size, matrix quality, and connectivity. Within parks and protected areas, habitat patch size can also be increased if turf or paved areas are converted to native plant gardens. In the urban matrix, native plants can be concentrated around existing large patches of greenspace, or to fill gaps in corridors. Local sourcing of native seed can protect genetic adaptation to local environments, and enhanced connectivity of native plants through the urban environment can promote gene flow and increase effective population sizes.

2. Plant a diversity of native plants to provide year-round resources. Supplying native plants that provide resources (such as flowers for pollinators) throughout the year can help to support a higher diversity of wildlife. The timing of seasonal production of flowers and fruit by native plants is also more likely to be aligned with migratory patterns and needs of native wildlife.

3. Remove and replace non-native vegetation with native plants. Areas of turf grass that are not used for heavy recreation, front yards, or sidewalk edges all provide opportunities for replacement with complex native vegetation.

4. Plant and manage host-specific plant species. Proactive management of species with known host-specific links to animals can benefit populations of these species. For example, milkweeds can be planted to support Monarchs, and native oak trees can be planted in groves to support acorn woodpeckers, cynipid wasps, and the many other oak specialist species that accompany them (Spotswood et al. 2017).

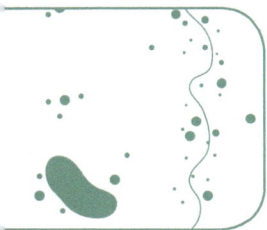

ELEMENT 06:
SPECIAL RESOURCES

DEFINITION
Unique habitat features necessary to support species' life history requirements, including large trees, wetlands, streams and rivers.

Background and significance

Many species have specific habitat requirements, and may be less successful in cities if specific requirements are not met (Devictor et al. 2008, Herrmann et al. 2012). In some cases, specialized requirements may only occur during certain times of year, or during certain life stages. For example, many birds have generalized diets and behavior, but have specific nesting requirements that can only be met by certain features, such as cavities in trees. Two particularly important special resources are water and large trees. These features support large numbers of species, creating site-scale hubs of biodiversity, and even a garden pond or a single large tree in a pocket park can be meaningful for species (Gaston et al. 2005, Stagoll et al. 2012).

All species rely on water, and in the urban landscape, water features are associated with greater biodiversity (Beninde et al. 2015). Urban water bodies serve as important hubs for both terrestrial and aquatic species (Hill et al. 2017). Ponds can serve as stepping stones of connectivity for insects and amphibians (Gledhill et al. 2008), and are also important for terrestrial organisms (Gaston et al. 2005). Large trees serve as the foundation for a local ecosystem on a small scale, providing large canopies and woody debris for shade and cover, cavities for nesting, flowers and fruits for forage, and litter that fertilizes soil (Stagoll et al. 2012).

Where special resources are not present, analogous features can sometimes serve a similar role (Lundholm and Richardson 2010). For example, cavities in trees are often limited in urban areas because large trees are rare (Roman and Scatena 2011) and dead limbs are proactively removed. Other types of valuable nesting habitat, such as ground cover, natural debris piles, and rock crevices are often lost during development, or are often highly modified. Artificial structures can help fill this void, providing habitat for a variety of organisms. Infrastructure such as bridges, culverts, buildings and utility structures, provide habitat for many bird species and bats (Keeley and Tuttle 1999, Morelli et al. 2014). Nest boxes can effectively serve as substitutes for cavities, supporting reproduction in cavity-nesting birds (Hamerstrom et al. 1973, Milligan and Dickinson 2016). Well-designed, located, and maintained bird boxes have the potential to support native birds in cities (Jackson and Tate 1974, Lindenmayer et al. 2009, Charter et al 2010, Hedblom and Söderström 2012). Certain nest boxes can also support native bees, and dead wood piles in gardens can support other insects and native reptiles (Gaston et al. 2005, Garden et al. 2007).

(Photo courtesy of Brocken Inaglory, CC by 2.0)

Who benefits from special resources?

Water benefits most wildlife and many plants. In cities, water bodies can support aquatic species that will not otherwise occur in the urban landscape, including aquatic invertebrates, amphibians, and fish. Water is also critical for most terrestrial wildlife, though in urban landscapes, urban-tolerant species may be the most common users.

Large trees can support a wide variety of species as well. Many insects may benefit from large masses of flowers or fruits (Cornell 1985, Stagoll et al. 2012). Bee hotels can create nesting habitat for native solitary bees. Other terrestrial insects, amphibians and reptiles, can find habitat in woody debris piles and other artificial structures with crevices. Nest boxes for birds can benefit some cavity nesting birds, though they should be designed, located and maintained carefully to manage for native species. Bridges can serve as roosting and nesting sites for swallows and bats.

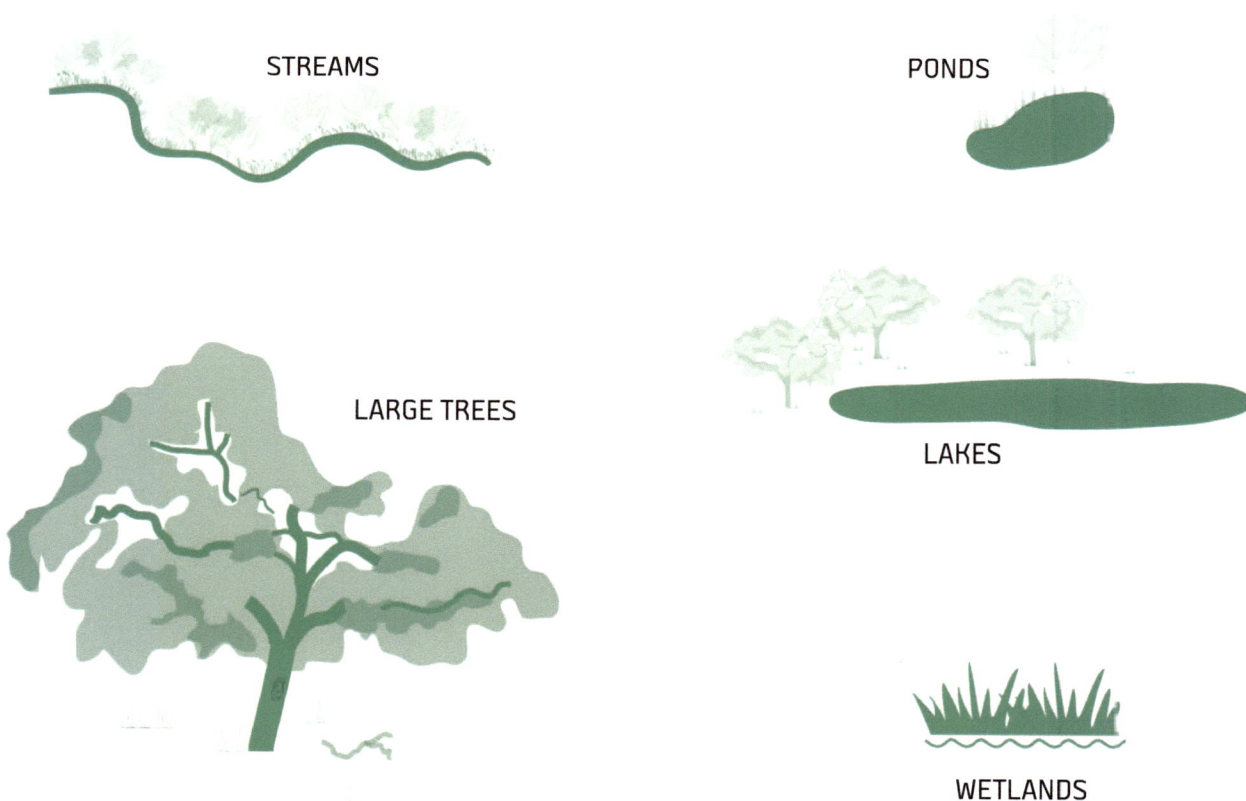

STREAMS

PONDS

LARGE TREES

LAKES

WETLANDS

Guidelines:

1. Protect, improve, and create new water features. Protecting wetlands and stream corridors can be achieved through riparian setback policies and statewide and federal wetland protection regulations. Some examples of new water features can include retention basins, small ponds, or bird baths and fountains. Even small mud puddles have benefits to some butterfly species during the dry season.

2. Protect, maintain, and plant large native trees. Large native trees should be protected and proactively maintained where they already exist, in recognition of the unique role they play in supporting biodiversity. Protecting large trees on private and public property can be accomplished through city-wide tree ordinances, urban forest management plans, and other policy mechanisms. Planting trees that will become large over time will help ensure the continued presence of large trees in the future.

3. Create and protect structures that support nesting and other life functions. Nest boxes, insect hotels, and bat boxes can be used to support cavity nesting birds, native bats and bees, arboreal mammals, and other organisms. These features can be modified in their design to better support native species (Jokimaki 1999, Cates and Allen 2002, Remacha and Delgado 2009).

(Photo courtesy of Phillip Shoffner, CC by 2.0)

ELEMENT 07:
MANAGEMENT

DEFINITION
Human activities and planning that promote positive biodiversity outcomes.

Background and significance

Improving the ways humans manipulate the landscape can help support more species in cities. From park maintenance to homeowner yard management to building design, a wide variety of human actions can influence biodiversity (Beninde et al. 2015). Among the many management actions that can benefit biodiversity, strategic stewardship of vegetation can improve its habitat value. Avoiding pruning trees and shrubs during bird and mammal breeding seasons can help reduce the impact of these activities on local wildlife (Hails and Kavanagh 2013). Retaining dead trees and branches can support cavity-nesting animals (Sandström et al. 2006), and these resources are particularly important given their rarity in urban landscapes (Stagholl et al. 2012). Leaving fruit and seeds on the ground can also increase food availability for local wildlife.

Promoting soil health is also an important component of managing for biodiversity. Soil compaction, degradation, and fill are common in cities, and can impede native vegetation communities from establishing. Improving soil quality through mulching, soil decompaction, or other interventions can benefit native plants and the animal communities that depend on them (Costello et al. 2011, Fite et al. 2011, Shwartz et al. 2015). Retaining leaf litter on the ground can also improve soil health and nutrient cycling, and fallen and decaying leaves and logs can also provide habitat (Gaston et al. 2005). Metal concentrations and water availability are also often modified in urban environments, and managing these inputs can help promote native plants over non-natives.

Reducing the area covered by lawns and changing how they are managed can also help support biodiversity. Lawns require frequent upkeep, including mowing, irrigation, chemical fertilizers and pesticide addition, and are often composed of only a few non-native species. These management inputs tend to reduce biodiversity (Aronson et al. 2017) and are resource-intensive, with particularly acute costs in arid and semi-arid ecosystems. Replacing lawns with more drought-tolerant native vegetation can increase plant and animal biodiversity while reducing other impacts, such as water demand and pesticide use (Donofrio et al. 2009). Where lawns are desirable for recreation and social gathering, reducing the use of fertilizers and pesticides as well as the frequency of mowing will help reduce their negative impacts on biodiversity (McKinney 2006, Lerman et al. 2018).

Beyond vegetation management, other stressors that limit biodiversity in cities include noise, light pollution, and chemical pollution in local soils and waterways. Pesticides, in particular, can adversely impact biodiversity (Shwartz et al. 2013). Urban infrastructure also creates challenges for plants and animals. Vehicle traffic leads to roadkill and noise that disturbs bird communication (Cardoso 2014). Reducing vehicle speed and adding trees near roadways can reduce wildlife mortality and noise impacts (Fang and Ling 2003, Hobday and Minstrell 2008). Street and building lighting can be modified to reduce impacts on nocturnal animals (Longcore and Rich 2004). Windows on buildings can also be designed to improve visibility to birds (Erickson et al. 2005).

Interactions with other species can also impact biodiversity in cities as well. Urban-adapted or invasive species may have negative impacts on native biodiversity through predation (Shochat et al. 2006, Rodewald and Gehrt 2014), competition (Faeth et al. 2005), and disease exposure (McCleery et al. 2014). For example, domestic cats can be prolific predators that limit bird populations (Loss et al. 2013). Managing to control pests, pathogens, and invasive species can help alleviate the negative impacts on native biodiversity (Bradley and Altizer 2007, Shochat et al. 2010). Management practices often follow seasonal climatic and ecological cycles. Land managers can strategically plan their interventions to limit ecological impacts (see Management section in Chapter 3 for an example).

Who benefits from management?

Managing for biodiversity has the potential to benefit a wide range of organisms. Reduced use of harmful pesticides will promote insect diversity and help support the birds that prey on them, while improved water quality in downstream creeks and rivers can enhance aquatic food webs. Tree-nesting birds and ground-dwelling wildlife will thrive with biodiversity-focused vegetation management. Managing domestic cats and feral cat colonies will aid most bird species, and particularly ground-nesting birds. Many ground-dwelling animals will have higher survival where road and vehicle management reduces traffic speeds and barriers. Wildlife-friendly lighting can support nocturnal animals such as moths and migratory birds. Native plant populations can also benefit from biodiversity-friendly management, and can indirectly support additional species.

Downed logs

Leaf litter

Bird-safe windows

Bird & bat nests

Limit light pollution

Minimize lawns

Reduce chemical inputs

Support healthy soils

Guidelines:

1. Manage vegetation to mimic natural structure and form. Maintain the integrity of vegetation and leave organic materials on the ground, including logs and branches. In large open spaces where pedestrian traffic is minimal, maintain dead trees on the landscape. Reduce frequent mowing, and if possible, maintain clippings on the ground in areas where mowing is necessary. Consider nesting season and nest or den sites when designing vegetation management plans.

2. Control invasive and urban-adapted nuisance species, pests, and pathogens. Manage invasive species through active restoration. Promote screening programs for diseases in animals and key vectors at plant nurseries and other centers of biotic transport, such as animal shelters, pet shops, and trading ports. Vaccinating domestic pets and wildlife at rehabilitation centers and treating with antiviral or anti-parasitic drugs can reduce exposure and transmission of pathogens to wildlife.

3. Mitigate and reduce pollutants and chemical inputs. Reduce the use of chemical inputs, including pesticides, chemical fertilizers, rat poison, and other pest control chemicals, particularly near water sources.

4. Target management in large, regionally significant corridors and biodiversity hubs. Prioritizing management for biodiversity may be most possible in large regional corridors and parks, where planning can integrate biodiversity management as a key priority. Mitigating stressors can be accomplished by creating wildlife crossings or closing roads during certain times of year, reducing vegetation management during sensitive periods, and leaving leaf litter, dead trees, and dead branches in place in areas with little foot traffic.

5. Design infrastructure to be wildlife-friendly. Reduce noise pollution by adding sound barriers and trees along roads. Promote the use of bird-friendly window design. Mitigate light pollution by dimming or turning off lights at night, using shields on street lights, and using green/blue night lights on buildings to reduce disorientation of birds (Ogden 1996, Poot et al. 2008). §

3 CASE STUDY:
SILICON VALLEY

Introduction

The region we think of as Silicon Valley lies in a densely urbanized valley (approximately 270 square miles) made up of several cities in Santa Clara County, California. Like many urban areas, the landscape is highly fragmented, crisscrossed by freeways, and covered by roads, buildings, and other infrastructure that pose many challenges for biodiversity. However, Silicon Valley also contains significant areas of habitat, particularly along creek corridors and in open spaces. Local biodiversity data show that Silicon Valley has a diverse community of plants and animals. Existing biodiversity, distributed through open spaces, backyards, urban trees, and other spaces can form the foundation from which to build more effective support for biodiversity.

Silicon Valley's sprawling suburban neighborhoods, mixed with commercial and industrial development, share similarities with many urban areas in the United States, making it an ideal case study for applying the elements outlined in Chapter 2 to a real landscape. A critical first step is to identify data sources that can show where existing biodiversity resources lie. In this chapter, we use Silicon Valley as an example to demonstrate how local data can be used to identify each element on the landscape. In any landscape, this process will likely lead to new insight about the region's support for biodiversity, and generate many ideas relevant for the biodiversity planning process.

It is also helpful to explore the history and trajectory of a place to understand its current potential — including which habitats the landscape used to support and how the physical and ecological patterns that underpin these ecosystems have changed over time. We begin this chapter by providing a brief

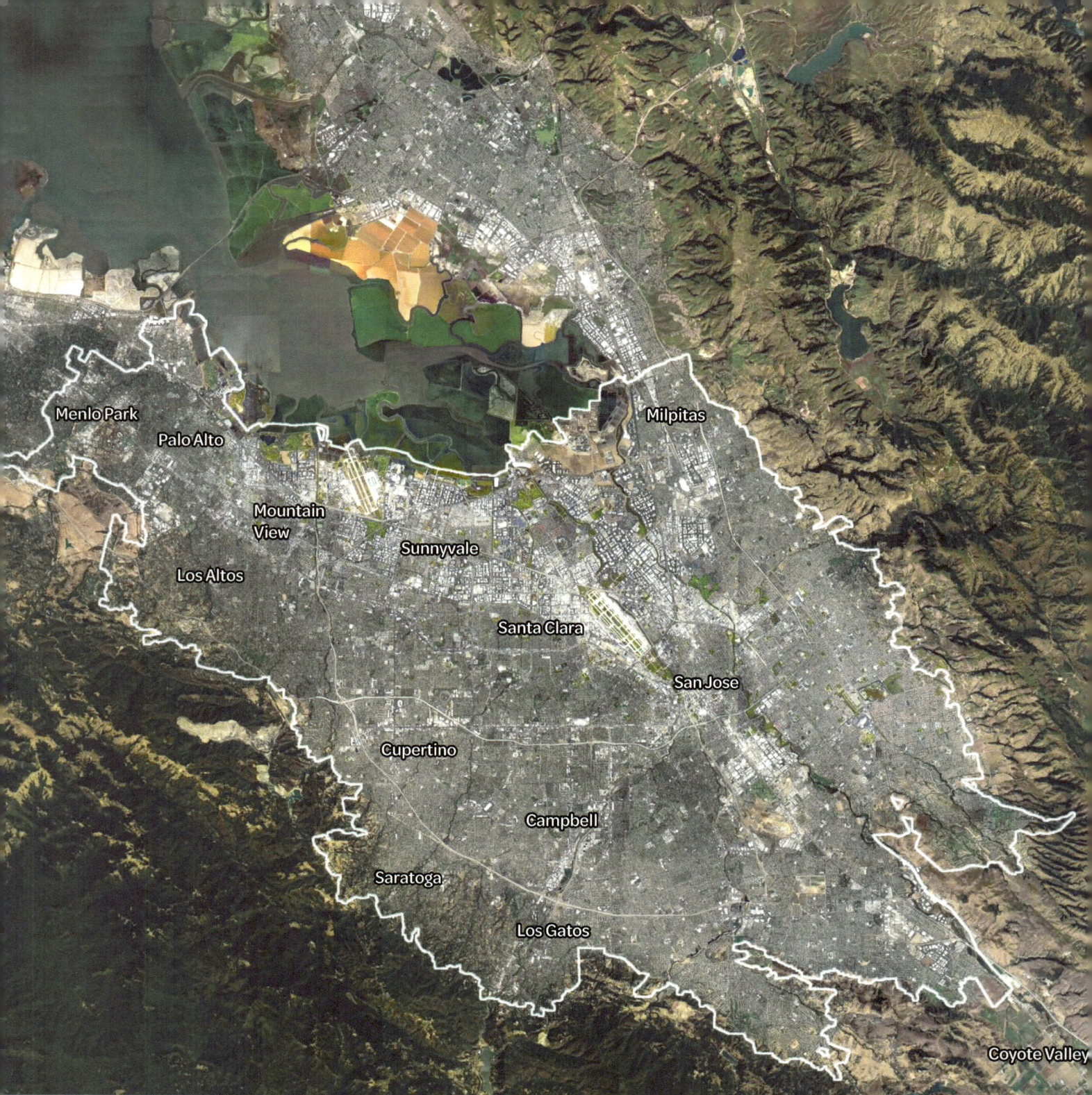

Menlo Park

Palo Alto

Mountain
View

Los Altos

Sunnyvale

Santa Clara

Milpitas

San Jose

Cupertino

Campbell

Saratoga

Los Gatos

Coyote Valley

N

Silicon Valley in context

5 miles

URBAN SILICON VALLEY

Figure 3.1 The region we know of as Silicon Valley (also called Santa Clara Valley), and its major cities, lie in Santa Clara County. To the north lies the San Francisco Bay. The Santa Cruz Mountains lie to the west and south, and the Diablo Range to the east. Coyote Valley to the south is a landscape of agriculture and ranches that serves as a critical wildlife linkage connecting the two mountain ranges.

overview of Silicon Valley's environmental, ecological, and land use history to help provide this context. We then draw on regional data to highlight how the seven elements of the Urban Biodiversity Framework can be applied to Silicon Valley. Cities are of course extremely diverse and complex, with unique histories, land-use legacies, environmental and socio-economic contexts, and a multitude of other factors. Because of this complexity, the process of applying the elements will vary across different cities. Chapter 4 outlines general approaches for using data-driven insights to develop a cohesive urban biodiversity strategy across land use types in any city.

Silicon Valley History and Change

Silicon Valley (also called Santa Clara Valley) lies between the Diablo Mountain Range to the east and the Santa Cruz Mountains to the west. Like the rest of the San Francisco Bay Area, Silicon Valley's climate is Mediterranean with mild, rainy winters and warm, dry summers. Nestled between these two mountain ranges, the valley experiences both hotter temperatures (average summer highs above 80° F [NOAA 2019]) and less rainfall (average annual precipitation 14 inches [Galloway et al. 1999]) than the cooler, damper climate of San Francisco to the northwest.

The valley floor was historically defined by well-drained alluvial soils near the foothills and more poorly-drained clay soils with high groundwater closer to the Bay. Soil conditions and groundwater have been significantly altered in many areas: artificial fill overlays clay soils in many places near the shore, and development has compacted and altered soils through much of the urbanized valley. Largely due to pumping for agriculture, groundwater levels dropped precipitously during the nineteenth century, causing localized subsidence in many places. In the last several decades, groundwater and subsidence have been stabilized by reduced pumping and recharge (Galloway et al. 1999).

Transformed over the past two centuries into the hub of technological innovation we know today, the urban landscape of Silicon Valley bears little resemblance to the historical landscape of vast oak woodlands, chaparral, and creeks that terminated in wet meadows and tidal marshes. Over the coming decades, Silicon Valley is expected to go through yet another transformation. Job growth over the next 20 years is projected to lead to substantial increases in population (McKenzie et al. 2017). Developed largely as low-density suburban housing during the decades after WWII, Silicon Valley will be challenged to accommodate this new growth, and will face pressure to increase density within the urban footprint and to develop into existing open space on the urban fringe (Karlinsky et al. 2017, McKenzie et al. 2017).

These economic and social drivers will put pressure on urban greenspaces that could be developed or transitioned to other uses, and could lead to changes that will support less biodiversity. However, these pressures will also present an opportunity: if we incorporate biodiversity and ecological resilience into plans for the future, we can create a Silicon Valley that benefits both people and nature. In shaping the biodiversity and resilience of the cities of Silicon Valley's future, we will create a model for better alignment between nature and people, both in California and beyond.

Land use and biodiversity planning

Silicon Valley today contains a diverse array of land uses. Suburban residential development covers the majority of the region, with commercial and industrial zones concentrated along major transportation corridors and in the lower-elevation areas fringing the Bay (Figure 3.2). The surrounding foothills support a patchwork of agriculture and open space, much of which is under local protection through regional park districts. Protected open spaces likewise encompass the majority of the land along the San Francisco Bay to the north of Silicon Valley.

Current zones of land use generally reflect ecological patterns in the valley that existed prior to major development. Stream courses still mostly mark their former locations, though many have been straightened and connected to the Bay. Oak savannas, woodlands, and patches of grassland and chaparral were once found on the well-drained alluvial soils that are now subdivisions. Expansive wetland habitats such as seasonal meadows, perennial wetlands, and willow groves were found across thousands of acres of flat, lower-lying areas (Beller et al. 2010). These areas remained undeveloped much later and still tend to support a lower density of industrial and commercial development than neighboring former oak groves (Grossinger et al. 2006, Grossinger et al. 2008, Beller et al. 2010, Spotswood et al. 2017).

The possibilities and suitability for urban biodiversity interventions in different parts of the region vary according to these land use types. For example, creating

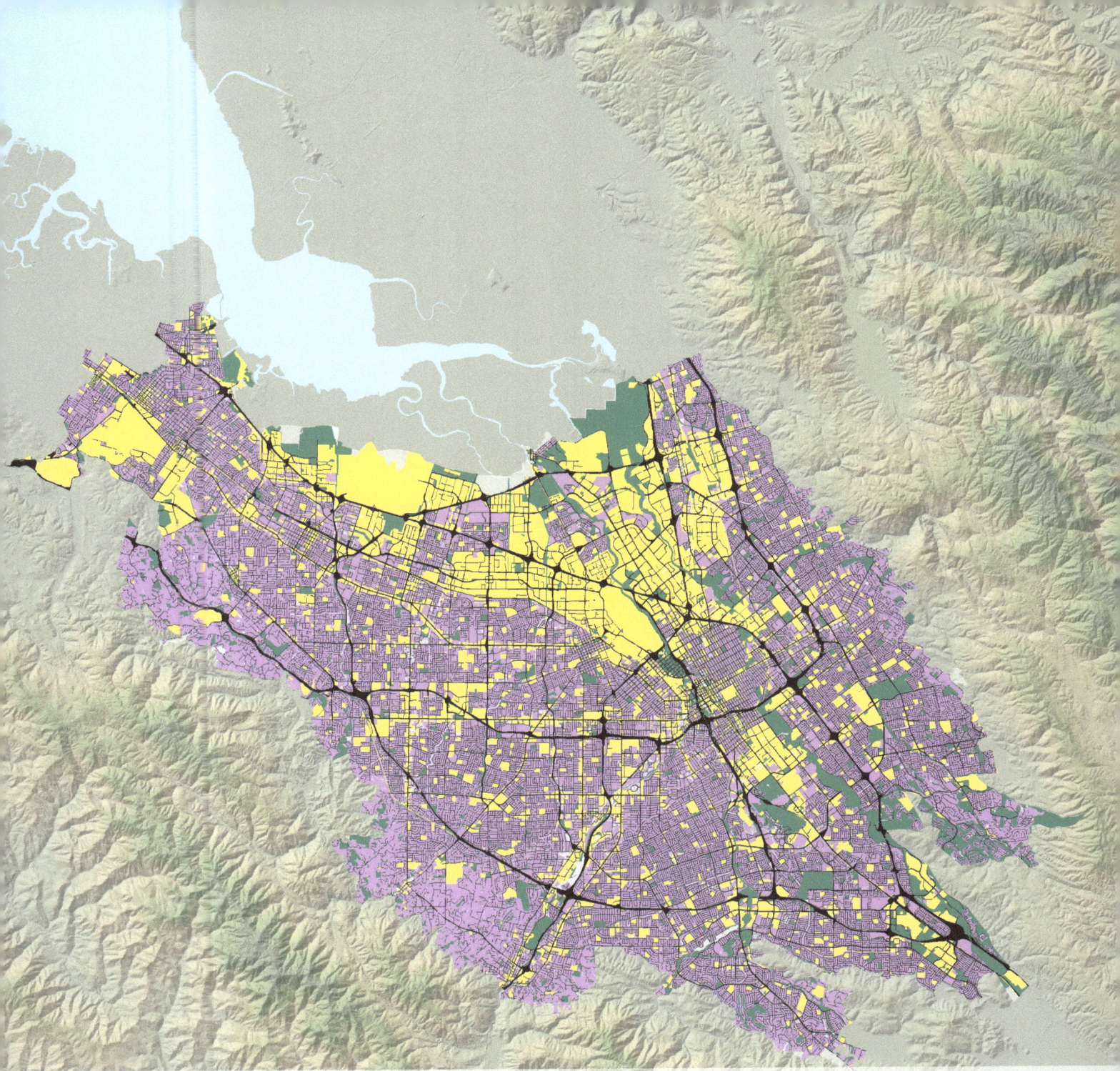

Silicon Valley **Land Use**

N

5 miles

- ▮ Commercial / Industrial / Institutional
- ▮ Open Space
- ▮ Residential
- ▮ Transportation Corridor
- ▯ Other

Figure 3.2 Residential land is the single biggest land use type in Silicon Valley . Commercial and industrial land use are concentrated near the Bay and close to transportation corridors (ABAG 2006). and major transportation corridors.

a small habitat patch on a residential property might involve converting lawn to native vegetation, whereas doing so along a transportation corridor could be accomplished by installing vegetated medians and green infrastructure. Similarly, variations within a given land-use type (e.g., different parcel sizes and owners) will also influence what actions make sense to prioritize where. In areas with high urban density, actions might be limited to native landscaping, while in low-density areas and open spaces, opportunities could include maintaining large trees and creating relatively unmaintained habitat patches.

Biodiversity in Silicon Valley

Silicon Valley lies within the California floristic province, a global biodiversity hotspot with both exceptional diversity and a high number of species endemic to the state (Baldwin 2014). California has both the highest plant and animal biodiversity in the country, and the second highest number of threatened species (Tershy et al. 2016). This statewide pattern is also evident in Silicon Valley (Bousman 2007, Baldwin et al. 2017).

While development has transformed the vast majority of ecosystems on the Valley's floor, the large protected areas in the adjacent hills and the Bay and the working landscapes of Coyote Valley to the south continue to provide significant habitat for plants and animals (Fig. 3.1). Unique endemic species such as the ridgeway's rail (*Railus obsoletus*) and bay checkerspot butterfly (*Euphydryas editha*), and habitats such as california sycamore (*Platanus racemosa*) alluvial woodlands and valley oak (*Quercus lobata*) woodlands are still found in pockets across the landscape. Santa Clara County supports hundreds of species of mammals, birds, reptiles, amphibians, and freshwater fish, as well as considerable native invertebrate and plant diversity (County of Santa Clara et al. 2012). While many of these species have populations concentrated in the hills, many also move through and use resources from the urban matrix. Some examples include native birds such as oak titmice (*Baelophus inornatus*), Anna's hummingbirds (*Calypte anna*), Bewick's wrens

(*Thryomanes bewickii*), and Nuttall's woodpeckers (*Picoides nuttallii*), or large mammals such as coyotes (*Canis latrans*) (eBird 2019, iNaturalist 2019).

The urban floor of Silicon Valley is distinct from the surrounding landscape, representing unique topographic, hydrological, and soil conditions that are not common in the surrounding hills or the Bay. To some extent, contemporary biodiversity patterns reflect the unique conditions found only on the valley floor. For example, willow flycatchers (*Empidonax traillii*) visit remnant patches of willow groves, now found primarily in flood detention basins in the urban landscape (eBird 2019). These willow groves were common historically on the valley floor close to the Bay, and remain to this day uncommon in the surrounding hills.

In the following pages, we draw on local datasets to identify existing biodiversity assets in Silicon Valley associated with each of the seven elements identified in Chapter 2. Drawing from local ecosystems, we identified focal species likely to benefit from interventions associated with each element. The selected species represent a range of taxonomic groups and life history traits such as habitat preference, home range size, mode of movement, and degree of habitat specialization. We also used local datasets to identify species that are able to tolerate urbanization, and thus most likely to benefit from biodiversity improvements in the urban landscape. Taken as a group, these species demonstrate how the elements can work together to create a set of actions likely to benefit a wide range of species that use the landscape in a variety of ways.

ELEMENT 01: PATCH SIZE

Regionally, the largest patches of habitat lie outside the urban core in extensive conserved open spaces surrounding Silicon Valley. To the north, Don Edwards National Wildlife Refuge and other preserves protect thousands of acres of wetlands along the San Francisco Bay. To the south and east, county parks and open space preserves conserve forests, grasslands, and chaparral in the Santa Cruz Mountains and Diablo Range. These large protected areas serve a critical role in supporting regional populations of native wildlife and plants, and also likely influence urban biodiversity. For example, some species move between urban and adjacent conserved landscapes daily or seasonally (Davis et al. 2012). For other species, occasional dispersal to the urban area from adjacent wildlands may allow the urban population to persist (Stacey and Taper 1992).

Within Silicon Valley's urban boundary, the majority of significant patches of habitat are contained within parks. Silicon Valley contains more than three hundred urban parks which range widely in size, intended use, and management authority. Cities manage most of the Valley's parks, from small neighborhood gardens and sports fields to larger preserves with oak woodlands, chaparral, and other native ecosystems. While the size of each park is a critical factor determining how much biodiversity it can support, it is not the only factor. Other factors like whether a park lies on a regional connectivity corridor, or if the park is managed for agriculture, can also have an impact. This means that some parks may over-perform relative to their size, while others may have less biodiversity than expected, given their size.

We used a California statewide database of protected areas (California Protected Areas Database) to identify habitat patches in Silicon Valley, and to categorize each by size using thresholds identified in Chapter 2 (see element Patch Size). Parks in the region range in size from two to over 250 acres, with the large majority between two and ten acres (Fig. 3.3). Some of these parks are highly isolated, separated by more than a mile from any other patch, while others close to the hills and to the Bay may benefit from proximity to adjacent large connected open spaces (Fig. 3.4). Protected areas along Silicon Valley's major stream networks may function as regional corridors with higher biodiversity (see Connections section). Other regions in the United States and abroad likely have analogous datasets of public lands (e.g. PAD-US) that allow for similar patch size analyses.

Distribution of Habitat Patch Sizes in Silicon Valley

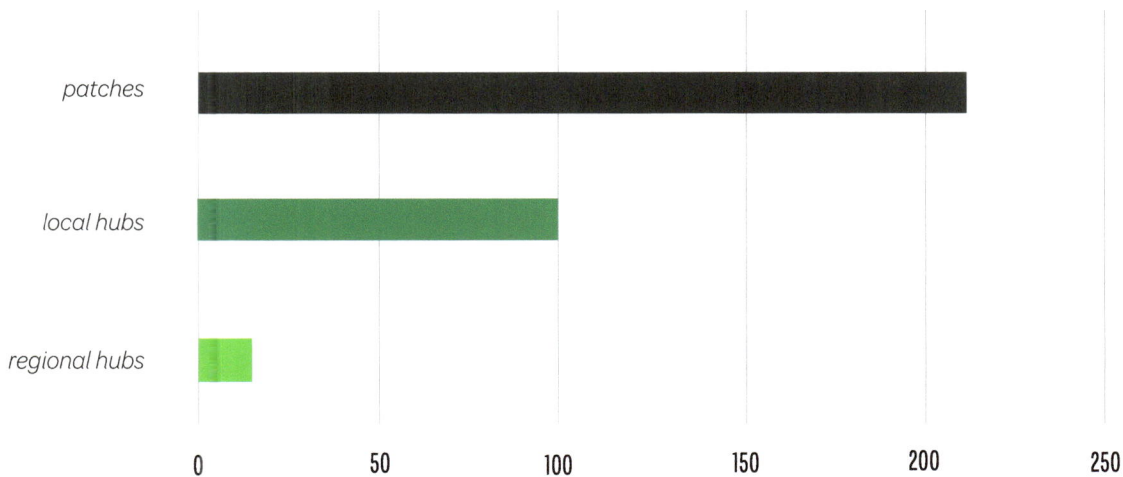

Figure 3.3 *Silicon Valley contains 326 open spaces, of which 212 are small habitat patches (2 - 10 acres) potentially suitable for species well adapted to urban environments. One hundred are local hubs (10 - 130 acres) potentially suitable for species somewhat sensitive to urbanization, and fourteen are regional hubs (130 acres or greater) that may harbor species found nowhere else in the urban landscape, such as those that are highly area sensitive or intolerant of cities. See appendix for more details.*

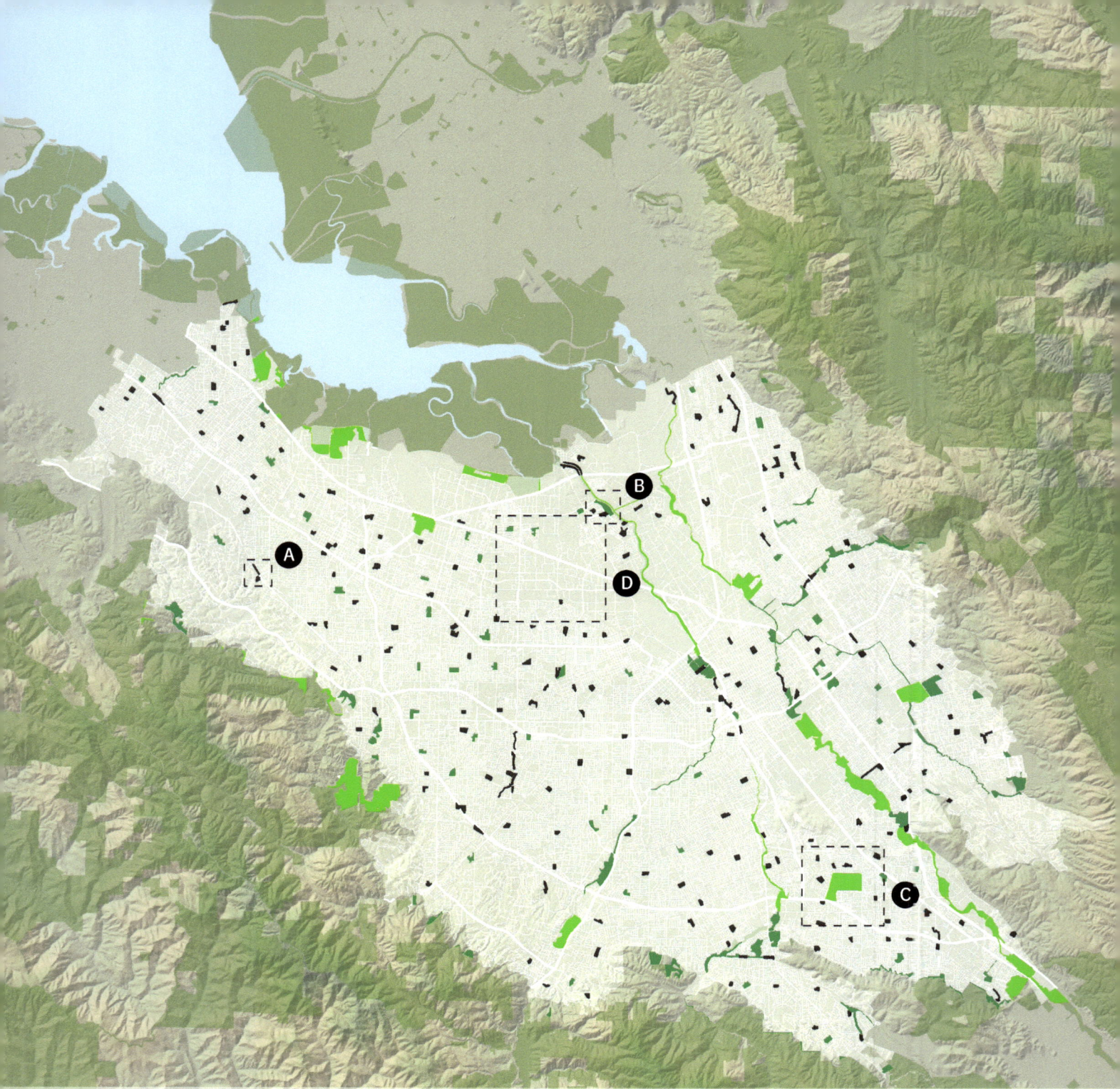

Silicon Valley Patch Size:

N

5 miles

■ **Patches**
(2 - 10 acres)

■ **Local hubs**
(10 - 130 acres)

■ **Regional hubs**
(>130 acres)

Figure 3.4 Small patches are relatively evenly distributed across the landscape of Silicon Valley, though there are areas that are relatively park poor. Regional hubs are rare, and many patches lie along regional connectivity corridors. Use of urban open spaces is not restricted to habitat protection and management, and the quality of habitat within each open space varies. Thus, the actual size required to support biodiversity in this region may vary.

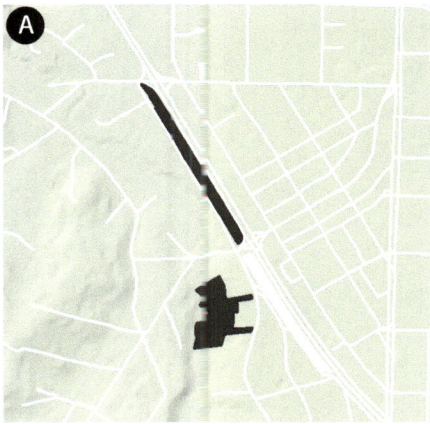

A. Small and isolated: Shoup Park in Los Altos is one of the many small isolated open spaces distributed across Silicon Valley. The four-acre park contains a redwood grove, a playground and a picnic area. It provides habitat mainly for urban-tolerant animal species, such as American robins (*Turdus migratorius*), Bewick's wrens, and California towhees (*Melozone crissalis*).

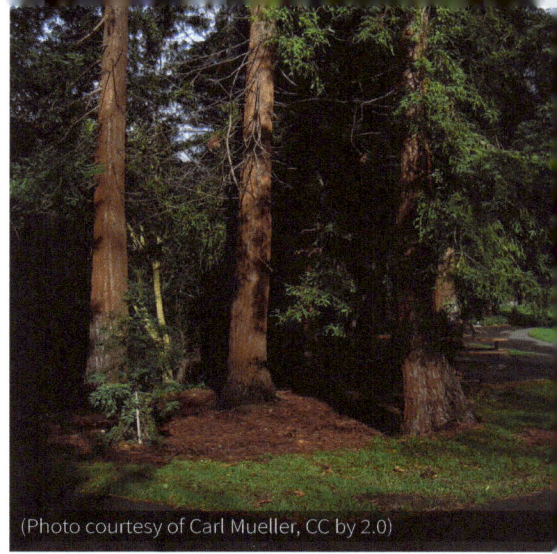

(Photo courtesy of Carl Mueller, CC by 2.0)

B. Connected patches: Ulistac Natural Area is a forty-acre preserve along the Guadalupe River corridor in Santa Clara containing acres of oak woodland, wetlands, and coastal scrub. Gray foxes (*Urocyon cinereoargenteus*) and jackrabbits (*Lepus californicus*) are seen often in the park, along with many other native animals. Birds include the urban-tolerant species found at Shoup Park, as well as some species that prefer less disturbed scrubland and forest interiors, such as ruby-crowned kinglets (*Regulus calendula*). It is one of only three urban parks in Silicon Valley that support California quail (*Callipepla californica), and b*iodiversity may be higher than its size suggests due to its location along a regional river corridor.

(Photo courtesy of JKehoe, CC by 2.0)

C. Large and managed: Martial Cottle park encompasses 287 acres of open space in San Jose. This large isolated park harbors a lower bird diversity than both Shoup Park and Ulistac, likely because it is managed for agriculture. Formerly a family ranch, croplands cover the majority of the park's area, with only sparse patches of native vegetation. The park provides habitat for species that tolerate frequent agricultural disturbance, such as Botta's pocket gophers (*Thomomys bottae*) and gopher snakes (*Pituophis catenifer*). Restoration to incorporate more native vegetation in the park may allow it to better act as a regional biodiversity hub.

(Photo courtesy of Don DeBold, CC by 2.0)

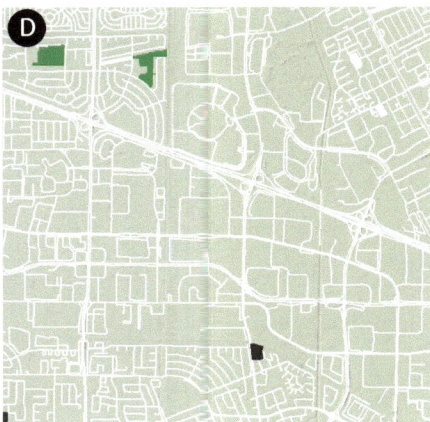

D. Park poor neighborhood: Northern Santa Clara containing acres of parking lots, busy streets, and office buildings, and few protected natural spaces. Buildings in the center of this region are over a mile from the nearest open space. This urban landscape poses a significant ecological barrier between the Bay to the north and hillsides to the south. Furthermore, residents of this area do not derive the health and psychological benefits that come from living within close vicinity of a greenspace.

(Photo courtesy of Gregory Varnum, CC by 2.0)

CALIFORNIA QUAIL

The California Quail (*Callipepla californica*) is a local example of an area-sensitive species (Bolger 2002). The charismatic bird lives in coveys (family groups) of up to seventy individuals that forage and raise young together. The quail's ground-dwelling behavior and nesting make it highly susceptible to predation and road fatalities. The species is thus rare or absent in urban environments with heavy vehicle traffic and abundant non-native predators. However, large urban parks with ample shrub cover and connections to regional biodiversity hubs do sometimes support quail. In Silicon Valley, visitors frequently report sightings of quail in Ulistac Natural Area, Almaden Lake Regional Park, and Hellyer County Park (eBird 2019, iNaturalist 2019).

(Photo courtesy of Melissa McMasters, CC by 2.0)

DIET: Quail eat seeds, grain, fruit, green vegetation, and insects. They require daily access to drinking water in hot weather.

HABITAT: Quail prefer a mixed habitat that includes low brush, trees, and grassland with adjacent water sources. They forage close to cover, take refuge in brush and trees, and nest in ground depressions beneath shrubs.

HOME RANGE: Evidence suggests that the winter home range of coveys varies between 17-45 acres, with an average of around 26 acres. During the breeding season, coveys dissolve and birds form pairs. During this time, home range sizes for pairs are smaller.

KEY STRESSORS: While quail populations are relatively stable outside of urban areas, habitat fragmentation, predation, and collisions with vehicles affect populations in cities and suburbs.

(Source: Zeiner et al. 1988, Birdlife International 2018, Cornell Lab of Ornithology 2019)

(Photo courtesy of Nikita Show, CC by 2.0)

Figure 3.5 *Area-sensitive species, like the california quail, may be confined to large habitat patches in the urban landscape if smaller patches are unconnected to regional corridors or to the urban edge.*

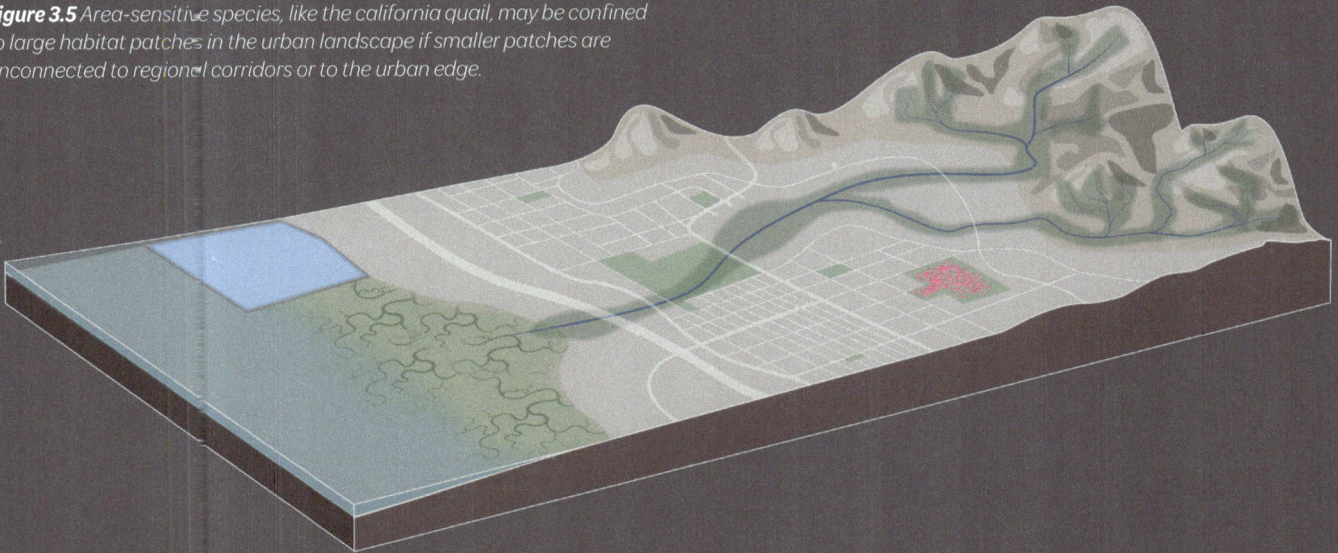

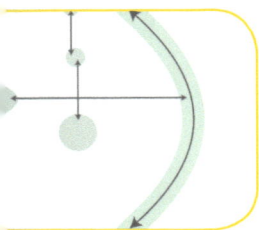

In Silicon Valley, connections between habitat patches take a variety of forms. Riparian zones along local creeks serve as the primary regional corridors that wind from parks in the hills, through cities, to the Bay. Some riparian zones, such as those along portions of Guadalupe River and Coyote Creek, contain large sections that are formally conserved through a network of city and county parks. Municipal zoning ordinances and general plan policies protect other riparian zones by forbidding development within a buffer zone around the corresponding waterway. The size of the buffer zone varies from city to city (San Francisco Bay Regional Water Quality Control Board 2004).

Silicon Valley has few other corridors to connect parks at a more local scale. Most parks are isolated by up to a mile from their nearest neighbors. While these parks may serve as stepping stones for species dispersing across the urban landscape, improving connections between them would likely greatly increase their ability to facilitate movement. Areas that are particularly park poor, such as in northern Santa Clara and Sunnyvale, contain few stepping stones or other connections.

While Silicon Valley has the underpinnings of a major corridor network in place, there are numerous opportunities for the region to fill gaps, broaden corridors, and remove barriers. None of the valley's riparian corridors is completely contiguous - many pass through culverts, have channelized segments with no vegetation, or segments engineered to run underground. Many are also extremely narrow, with little riparian vegetation. Meanwhile, arterial and neighborhood roads cut through Silicon Valley's local non-riparian corridors. Many barriers within the urban matrix preclude isolated parks from acting as stepping stones. Roads with heavy vehicle traffic pose high risk of animal mortality, and concrete parking lots and cultivated lawns may block species that require tree canopy or underbrush to traverse the landscape. Light and noise associated with urban activities may likewise deter animal crossings. Future planning to reduce or remove these barriers has the potential to benefit the wide variety of animals that pass through Silicon Valley.

We assessed habitat connectivity in Silicon Valley using data quantifying vegetation cover along waterways from the Santa Clara Valley Water District (SCVWD) and by analyzing the spatial distribution of protected areas in the region. Where similar vegetation surveys are currently unavailable or financially infeasible to conduct, planners may also assess habitat connectivity using aerial imagery.

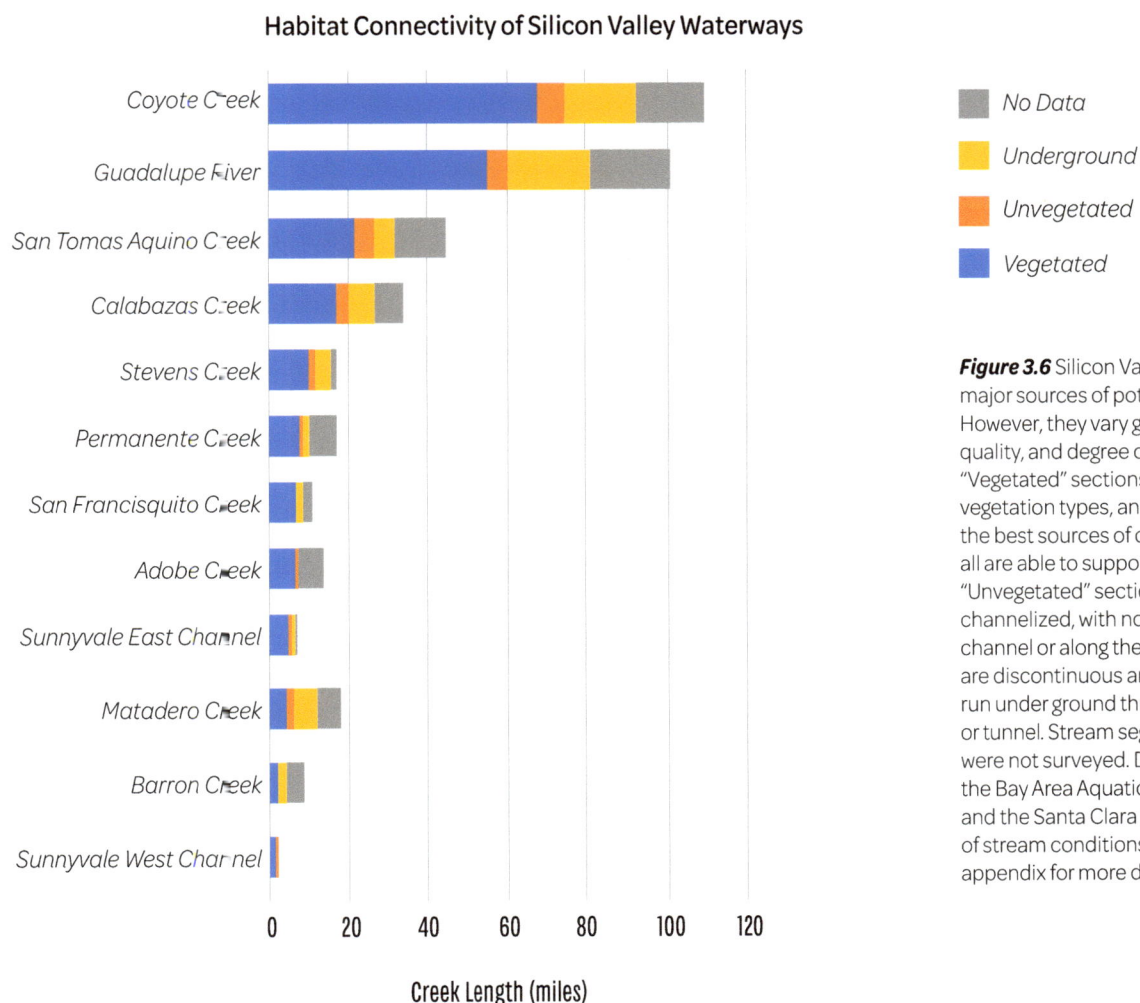

Habitat Connectivity of Silicon Valley Waterways

Legend:
- No Data
- Underground
- Unvegetated
- Vegetated

Creek Length (miles)

Figure 3.6 Silicon Valley's 12 waterways are major sources of potential connectivity. However, they vary greatly in size, habitat quality, and degree of modification. "Vegetated" sections contain a variety of vegetation types, and while they represent the best sources of connectivity, not all are able to support riparian trees. "Unvegetated" sections are typically channelized, with no vegetation in the channel or along the banks. "Underground" are discontinuous areas where streams run under ground through a large culvert or tunnel. Stream segments with "No data" were not surveyed. Data are taken from the Bay Area Aquatic Resources Inventory and the Santa Clara Water District surveys of stream conditions and vegetation. See appendix for more details.

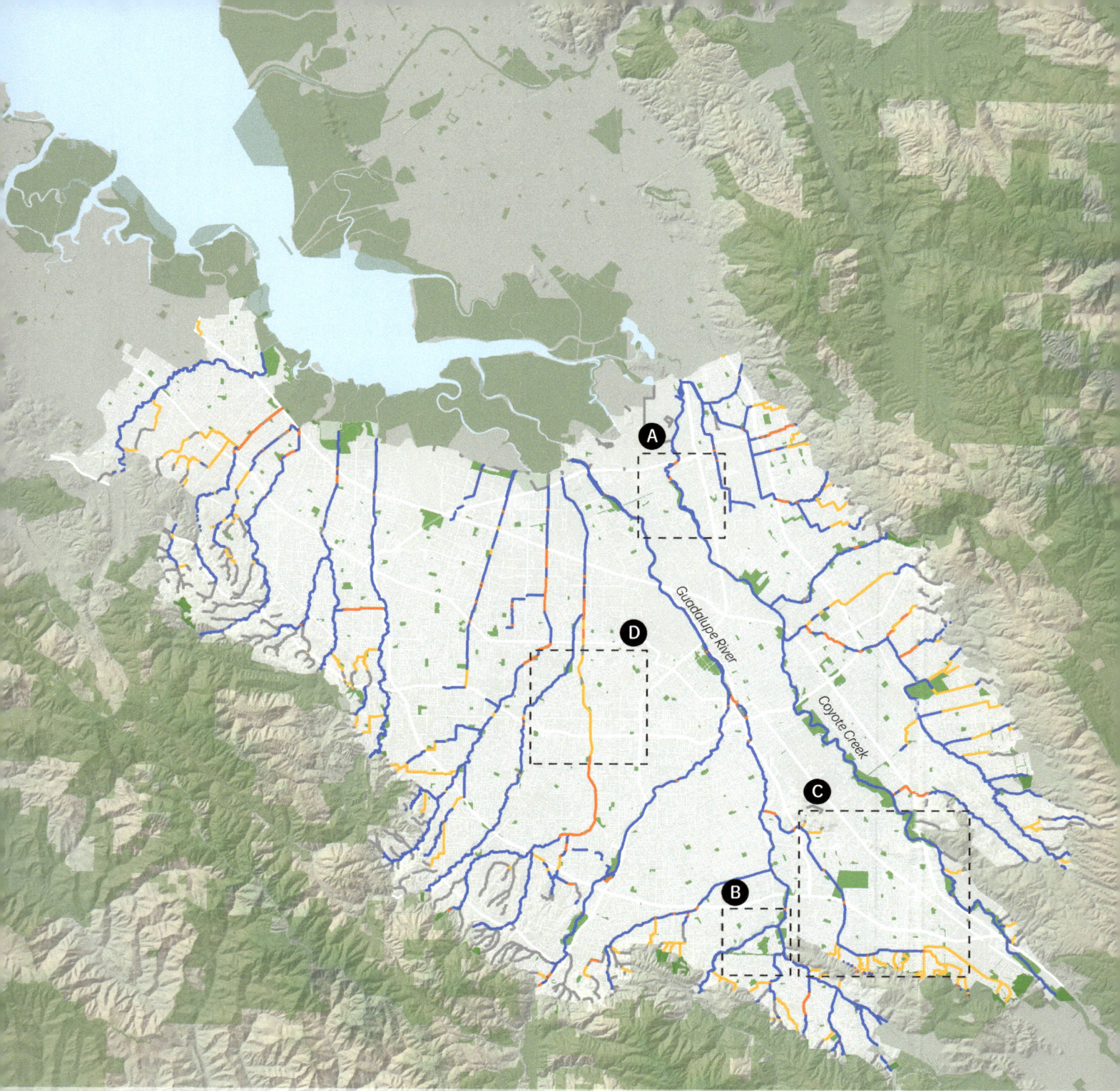

Silicon Valley Connections:
Stream Corridors

— Underground
— Unvegetated
— Vegetated
— No Data
Patches

N

5 miles

Figure 3.7 Opportunities for connectivity across the urban landscape come mainly from stream corridors. Most streams are not entirely connected, containing sections that have high potential to support connectivity ("vegetated") and sections that are disconnected ("unvegetated" or "underground"). Protected areas from the California Protected Areas Database and California Conservation Easement Database are also displayed to show connected blocs of dedicated open space. Shown with the current road network, this map highlights where future investments may be beneficial (i.e. in gaps in vegetated areas or open space blocs). See Figure 3.6 for more details on stream classification.

A. Chain of parks. Along Coyote Creek, a chain of parks winds through San Jose from Henry Coe State Park to the Bay, terminating at Don Edwards National Wildlife Refuge. While segments of the creek run underground or lack vegetation, Coyote Creek acts as the region's longest vegetated riparian corridor. Connected parks create wide habitat corridors in some sections, such as in Hellyer County Park (177 acres) and Shady Oaks Park (8 acres). Vegetation along the corridor provides cover for coyotes, brush rabbits (*Sylviagus bachmani*) and other wildlife recorded by visitors traveling along the creek (iNaturalist 2019).

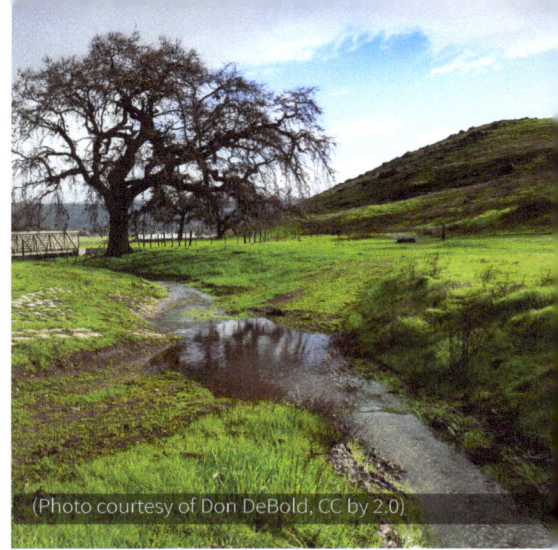

(Photo courtesy of Don DeBold, CC by 2.0)

B. Local greenway. TJ Martin and **Jeffrey Fontana Parks** form a greenway that serves as a 1.2-mile local, non-riparian corridor connecting Guadalupe Oak Grove park (58 acres) to a chain of parks along the Guadalupe river to the west and the Alamitos Creek riparian zone to the east. Wildlife recorded along the greenway include black-tailed deer (*Odocoileus hemionus*), California ground squirrels (*Otospermophilus beecheyi*), and oak titmice (*iNaturalist 2019*). These oak and grassland-associated species suggest this greenway serves as a source of connectivity to adjacent parks with larger patches of grassland and oak woodland habitat.

(Photo courtesy of Allan Hack, CC by 2.0)

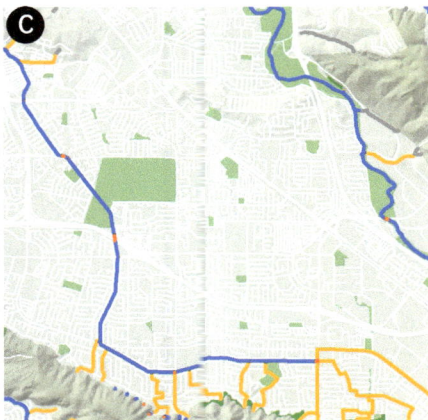

C. Stepping stones. The Edenvale neighborhood of San Jose contains a high density of parks where no two are more than one kilometer apart. More than 30 parks in this area vary in habitat quality, with some primarily composed of native ecosystems (e.g., Edenvale Gardens) and others containing sports and agricultural fields (e.g., Martial Cottle Park). Edenvale's parks may serve as stepping stones through the neighborhood, provided that the species can tolerate conditions within each park and in the surrounding housing developments. Brush rabbits and California ground squirrels are plentiful in the area and may fulfill these criteria (iNaturalist 2019).

(Photo courtesy of Martin Kalfatovic, CC by 2.0)

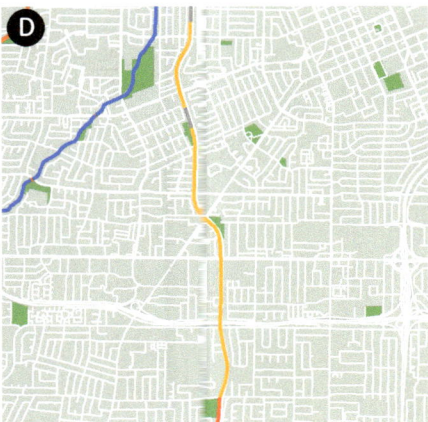

D. Large gap. San Tomas Aquino Creek drains from headwaters in El Sereno Open Space Preserve, north through Saratoga and Santa Clara, emptying to the Bay in Alviso. While the lower reaches of the creek support riparian vegetation, much of the creek is channelized and unvegetated. A 3.5-mile stretch runs entirely underground beneath the San Tomas Expressway. This section represents a large gap in the regional connectivity of this creek, and likely limits the ability of terrestrial animals to travel long distances.

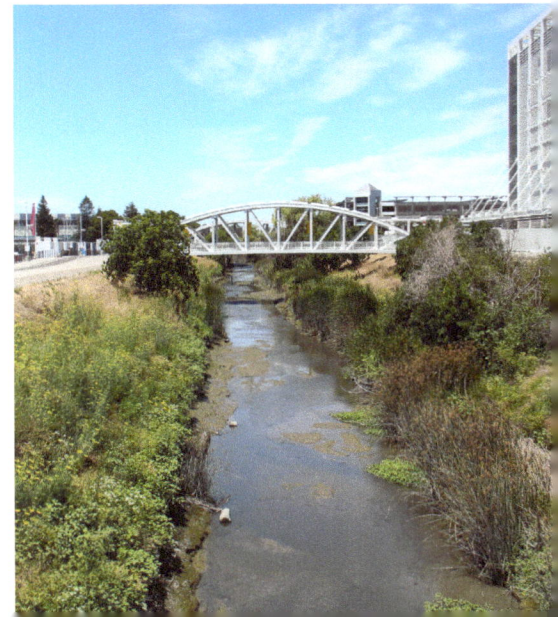

BOBCAT

Bobcats have large home ranges and are sensitive to urbanization, making them particularly able to benefit from large regional corridors. Common in the mountain ranges surrounding Silicon Valley, bobcats occasionally venture onto the valley floor. They traverse long distances across various ecosystems as they forage for prey, and a single individual may occupy a home range anywhere from 2 to greater than 20 square miles in size. In urban areas, bobcats preferentially travel along riparian zones and other corridors that provide continuous cover (Tigas et al. 2002). The Peninsula Open Space Trust has recorded bobcats traveling along the linked chain of parks along Coyote Creek, including in areas where the creek passes beneath major highways (Santa Clara Valley Open Space Authority and Conservation Biology Institute 2017). Such large-scale habitat connections allow bobcats to access open spaces in the urban interior while minimizing road crossings and other threats associated with the urban environment.

(Photo courtesy of National Park Service)

DIET: Bobcats are mostly carnivorous, with a diet that includes rabbits, rodents, deer fawns, birds, reptiles, and occasionally fruits and grass. They likely require regular access to water sources.

HABITAT: Oak woodland, conifer forest, and chaparral adjacent to riparian areas and denser forest. Dens in rock cavities, dead logs, stumps, and snags.

HOME RANGE: An individual may travel between 1.6 and 3 miles per day. Their home ranges average ten square miles in size.

KEY STRESSORS: Habitat loss, mortality from vehicles (Riley et al. 2003), competition with coyotes and other species, and predation by mountain lions and domestic dogs.

(Source: Zeiner et al. 1988)

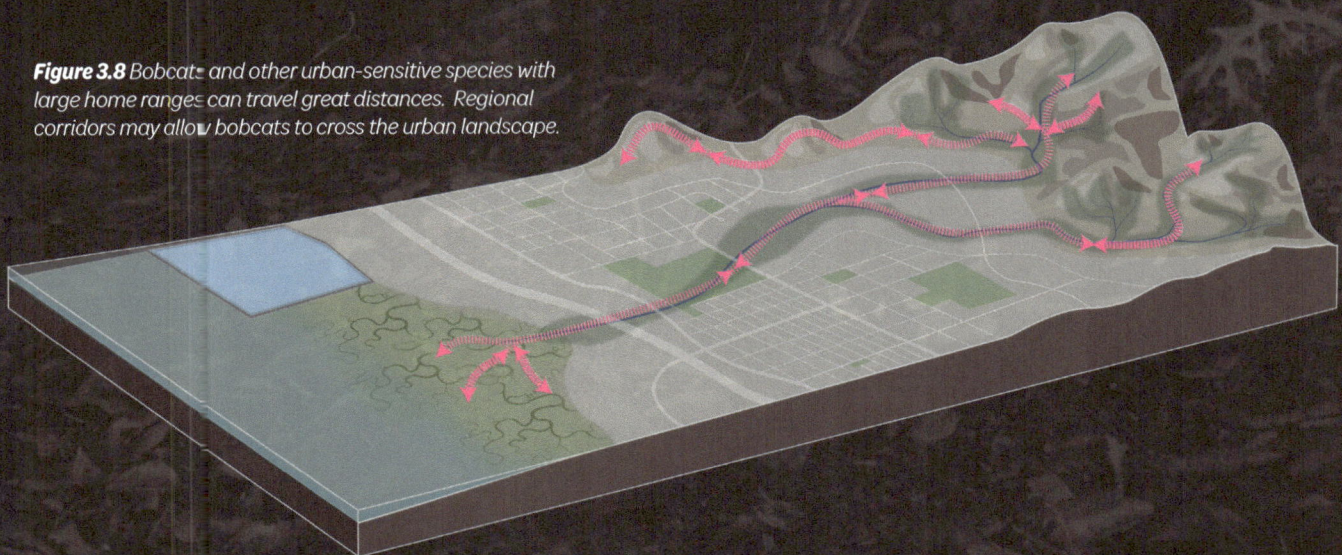

Figure 3.8 Bobcats and other urban-sensitive species with large home ranges can travel great distances. Regional corridors may allow bobcats to cross the urban landscape.

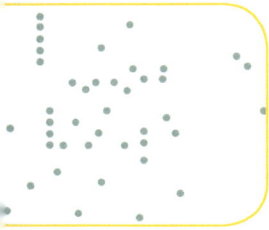

ELEMENT 03: MATRIX QUALITY

Silicon Valley's urban matrix outside open spaces and stream corridors is comprised of a patchwork of streets, houses, commercial buildings, and vegetation. Development has resulted in highly fragmented remnants of intact habitat of variable quality across the urban matrix. Given its large area, the urban matrix represents a sizable opportunity to conduct urban biodiversity enhancements.

While tree canopy cover is only one metric for quantifying matrix quality, it is widely available, easily measurable from remotely sensed imagery, and correlates with overall habitat quality in the urban matrix (Hodgson et al. 2007). In Silicon Valley, tree canopy is related to development patterns. Canopy is concentrated near the hills in areas of lower-density, residential land use (Figure 3.10). By comparison, downtown San Jose, at the center of the valley floor, has relatively low canopy cover, a higher density of impervious surfaces, and greater urban density.

As in many cities, tree canopy cover also tracks patterns of income (Schwarz et al. 2015). Higher canopy cover is concentrated in wealthier, lower density residential areas such as Palo Alto, Los Altos Hills, Saratoga and Los Gatos. Canopy cover is lowest in the most disadvantaged neighborhoods toward San Jose's core. These areas are potentially more vulnerable to the urban heat island effect, have greater exposure to air pollution, and are less able to provide other health benefits that come from trees (e.g, Hartig et al. 2014). When choosing sites for matrix quality improvements, existing disadvantaged neighborhoods that lack tree canopy can be prioritized for tree planting.

There are many opportunities to increase tree canopy in areas where trees are sparse. Trees and other vegetation can be installed along streets, in backyards, in schoolyards, or in parking lots in commercial districts (such as along El Camino Real). The Oakwell survey of the City of Palo Alto shows numerous large, native oak trees along city streets, in backyards, and in parking lots, providing an example for how a city can improve matrix quality using large native trees.

We used publicly available canopy cover data from the California Department of Forestry and Fire Prevention (CalFire 2015) to quantify matrix quality across Silicon Valley. These data are appropriate for similar analyses in urban areas throughout the state. For analyses elsewhere in the United States, the National Land Cover Database provides similar canopy cover data. Fine-scale land cover maps, where available, can also provide insight into matrix quality.

Canopy Cover by City

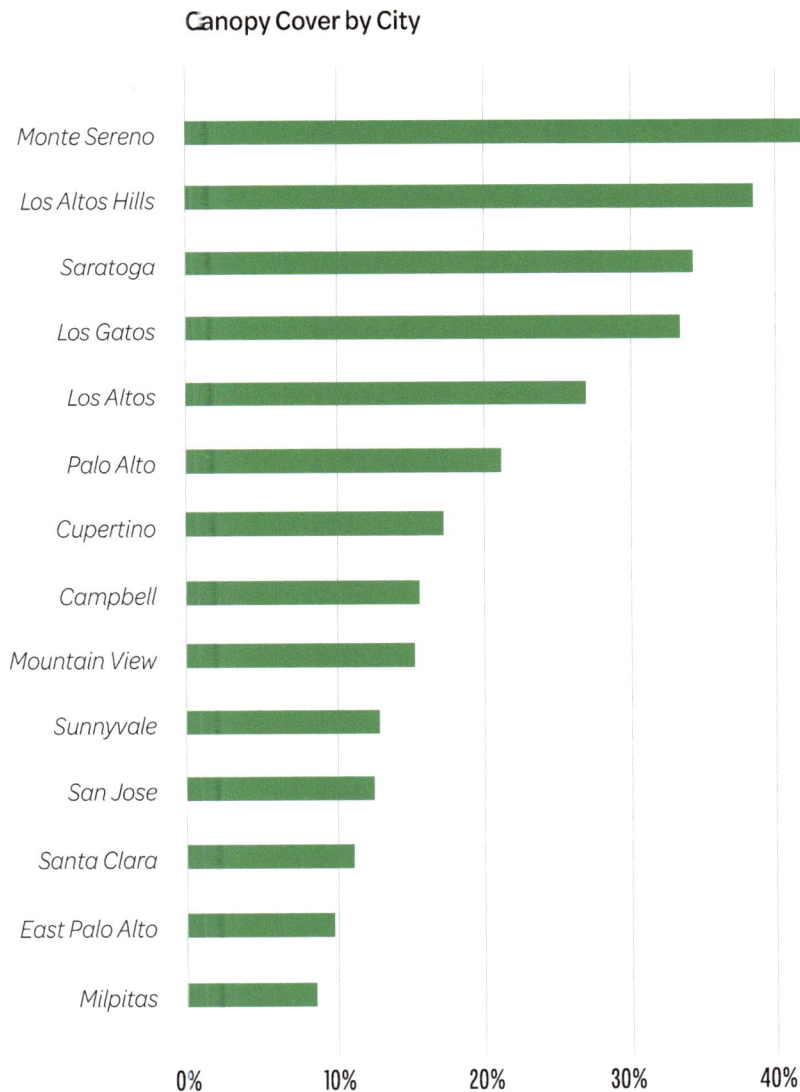

Figure 3.9 Tree canopy cover is highly variable among cities in Silicon Valley. Some of the cities with highest average canopy cover are also the most affluent in the region. Canopy cover data are calculated averages for each city (CalFire 2015). See appendix for more details.

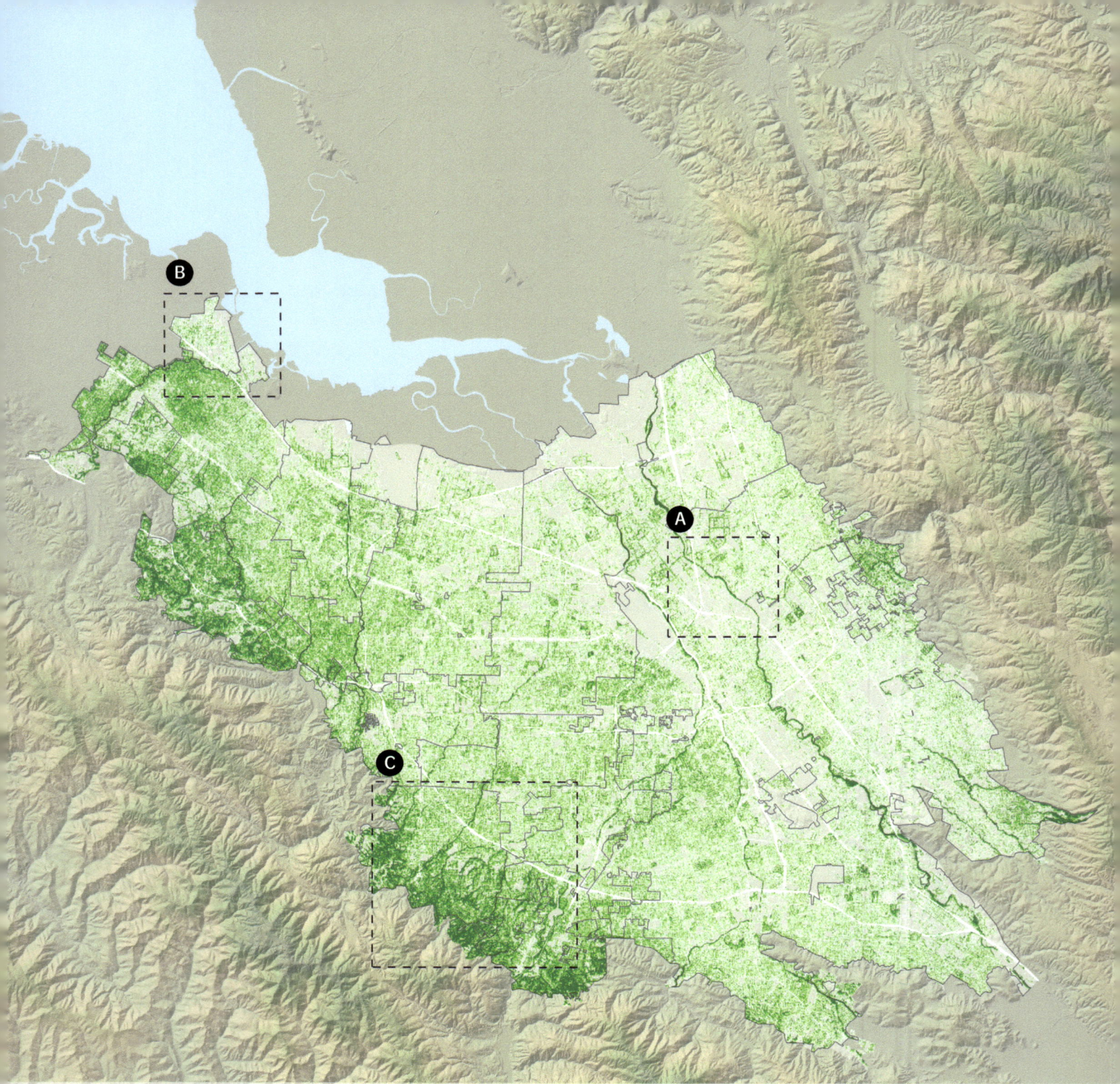

Silicon Valley Matrix:
Canopy Cover

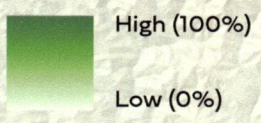

High (100%)

Low (0%)

N

5 miles

Figure 3.10 The distribution of tree canopy cover is one important measure of matrix quality. Darker shades of green represent areas more densely covered by trees. Areas lacking tree canopy cover can be found in some of the most disadvantaged communities in the county in downtown San Jose and in the commercial and industrial areas close to the Bay. Source: Calfire 2015.

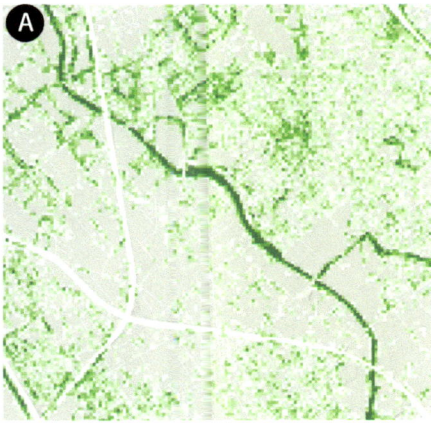

A. Treeless industrial neighborhood. North San Jose between Coyote Creek and Guadalupe River contains little vegetation or canopy cover. Industrial buildings and parking lots cover the majority of the land area. Given its location between Silicon Valley's two primary regional corridors, the area could support local connectivity between the two creeks if matrix quality were improved. Planting native trees and understory plants could benefit biodiversity, and could be achieved through coordination with the city and local businesses.

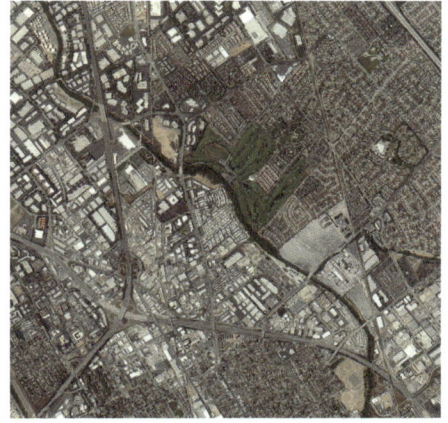

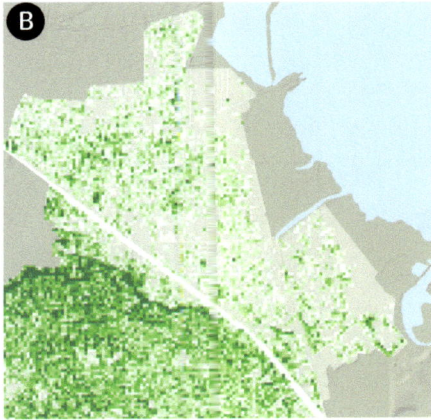

B. Disadvantaged city. The city of East Palo Alto contains significantly less canopy cover than neighboring cities. The majority of the community is made up of residents from racial minorities with a lower median income than many other cities in Silicon Valley. The disparity in canopy cover affects both biodiversity and East Palo Alto's residents, who are more likely to experience extreme heat and may not derive many of the other health benefits that come from living close to nature. This disparity can be reduced through coordination with the city and homeowners to plant trees and native vegetation on residential properties and along streets.

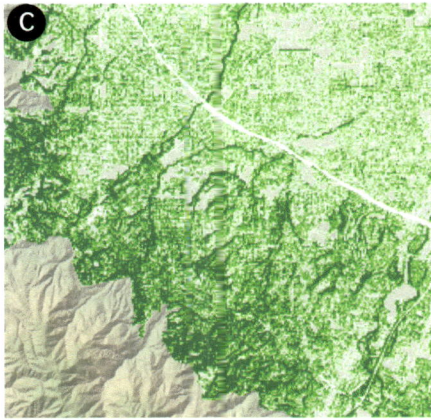

C. Wealthy cities with trees. Saratoga and Los Gatos contain some of the densest canopy cover in Silicon Valley. The relatively wealthy towns consist primarily of large residential properties, many with tree canopy levels comparable to those of neighboring open spaces in the Santa Cruz Mountains. Abundant vegetation in Los Gatos and Saratoga likely creates high-quality habitat for plants and animals. Homeowners can improve matrix quality by replacing non-native ornamental plants with native species, removing fences, and managing for biodiversity.

BLACK-TAILED BUMBLE BEE

The black-tailed bumble bee (*Bombus melanopygus*) is a common pollinator within parks, gardens, grasslands, and chaparral of Silicon Valley. Tolerant of urbanization, the species is abundant in urban areas (Hatfield et al. 2014). Black-tailed bumblebees have been recorded across neighborhoods in Silicon Valley, including East Palo Alto, Palo Alto, Mountain View, Cupertino, Los Altos, Saratoga, and San Jose (iNaturalist 2019). They have also been found in gardens in the suburban areas close to the hills.

Queen bees nest in cavities such as rodent holes and birds nests in urban parks and yards. The queen and worker bees forage for pollen and nectar from clover, sage, manzanita, and other flowering plant species around their nests. Installing potential nesting structures and cultivating bee-friendly gardens in residential landscapes can help support the black-tailed bumblebee.

(Photo courtesy of National Park Service)

DIET: Nectar and pollen from flowering plants, including *Ceanothus, Ericameria, Eriodyction, Eriogonum, Lupinus, Penstemon, Rhododendron, Salix, Ribes, Salvia, Trifolium, Vaccinium,* and *Wyethia.* Bees will visit a mixture of native and exotic flowers.

HABITAT: Bees forage in grassy areas, chaparral, shrubland, urban parks, and gardens. Queens will nest in rodent holes or bird nests.

KEY STRESSORS: Although the species has a stable population throughout its range, it is sensitive to habitat loss, pesticide use, disease spread from domestic bee hives, and competition with non-native bees.

A black-tailed bumble bee visiting california rose (*Rosa californica*) in a small area of native landscaping integrated into the De Anza Community College Campus.

(Sources: McFrederick and LeBuhn 2006, Hatfield et al. 2014, Bartomeus et al. 2016)

(Photo courtesy of Alejandro Dauguet, CC by 2.0)

(Photo courtesy of JKehoe, CC BY 4.0)

Figure 3.11 *Matrix improvements are particularly beneficial for pollinators. The black-tailed bumble bee will fly through the urban landscape to reach foraging patches. Improvements in the matrix include maintaining potential nesting structures and expanding food sources outside patches and corridors.*

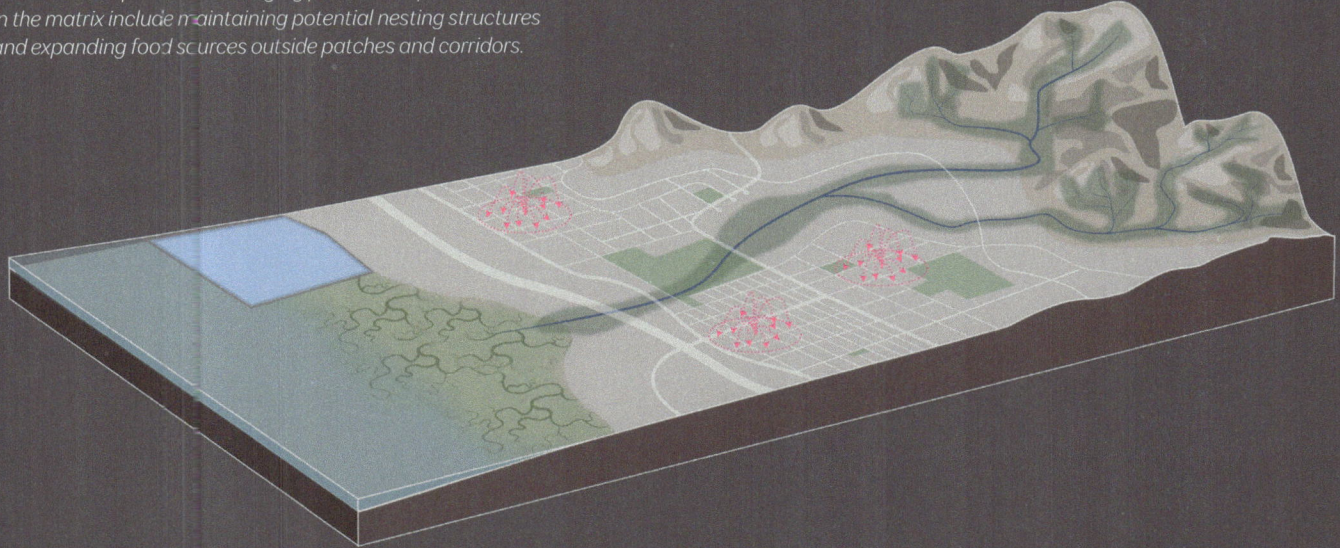

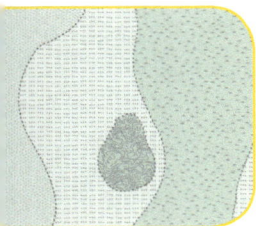

ELEMENT 04: HABITAT DIVERSITY

Like many urban areas, Silicon Valley has undergone fragmentation and homogenization that has eliminated much of its habitat diversity. Prior to European colonization, a complex mosaic of habitat types wove through the valley floor (Fig 3.12). Near the Bay, tidal marshes, seasonal wet meadows, and large willow groves flourished. On higher ground, oak woodlands covered much of the landscape, and native perennial bunch grasses and annual wildflowers thrived in neighboring grasslands. Riparian forests along creeks were characterized by California sycamores (Platanus racemosa), alders (Alnus spp), and Fremont cottonwoods (Populus fremontii) (Grossinger et al. 2006, Grossinger et al. 2008, Beller et al. 2010).

Today, non-native trees, lawns, and horticultural plants dominate much of the suburban and commercial areas of Silicon Valley. However, rare pockets of habitat persist. Cities such as Palo Alto and San Jose have tree ordinances that ensure the protection of large native oaks and other native trees. Parks and riparian buffer zones protect sections of the Guadalupe River and Coyote Creek, including patches of sycamore alluvial woodland and groves of cottonwood. Large parks have also preserved patches of oak woodland, particularly near the hills. In some places, patches of unique habitat types have appeared in new locations near where they were found historically. For example, small willow groves have colonized a network of flood detention basins along the Bay in the cities of Sunnyvale, Mountain View, Alviso, and Milpitas.

Remnant patches of persistent habitat can form the basis for habitat restoration efforts in Silicon Valley. These landscapes offer many opportunities where habitat zones could help create more functional and coherent patches of habitat within the urban matrix. For example, homeowners can replace lawns with mixtures of shrubs, small herbaceous vegetation, leaf litter, and logs to mimic the spatial and vertical complexity of oak woodlands that were once common on the valley floor.

Silicon Valley's historical mosaic of habitat types is a useful foundation for the development of habitat zones to guide planning for both the present and the future. While historical ecology can guide what habitats could be appropriate for current conditions, the information should be supported by other contemporary information and climate change predictions. Modifications to the physical landscape at the site scale, such as through irrigation, construction fill, or groundwater pumping, can alter which habitats are feasible to re-create. In addition, climate change will alter which habitats and species will do well in which locations. Where historical ecology information is lacking, habitat zones can be developed using information about contemporary physical and environmental gradients. Local ecological knowledge can help link physical gradients to habitat types to make a best guess about which types of habitats will be most appropriate.

Willow groves have spontaneously colonized flood detention basins close to where they were common historically. These willow groves support a high diversity of birds, including willow flycatchers and other neotropical migrant songbirds that are known to use them as stopover sites during migration. This unique habitat is only found where groundwater is high, and they are not common outside urban areas in the Bay Area. Their presence in urban areas creates a unique habitat type that increases regional habitat diversity.

(Photo courtesy of Shira Bezalel)

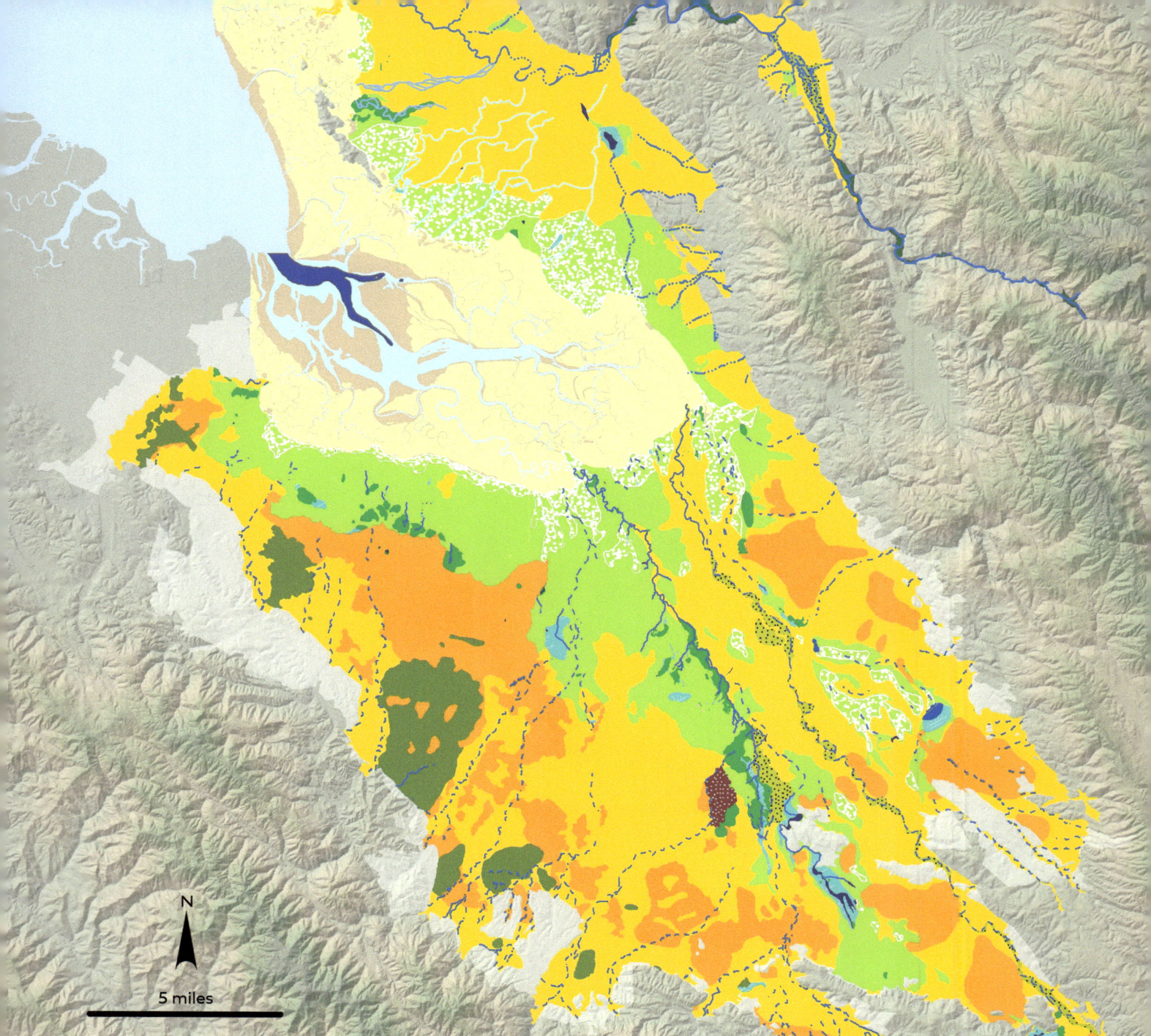

Silicon Valley
Historical Habitat Diversity

- Alkali Meadow
- Box Elder Grove
- Chaparral
- Oak Savanna / Grassland
- Oak Woodland
- Perennial Freshwater Pond
- Seasonal Lake / Pond
- Valley Freshwater Marsh
- Wet Meadow
- Willow Thicket
- Sycamore Alluvial Woodland, Riparian Scrub, Unvegetated Riparian

- Perennial Channels
- Intermittent Channels
- Tidal Marsh
- Tidal Mudflat
- Shallow Bay
- Deep Bay

N

5 miles

Figure 3.12 Before development, Silicon Valley contained a mosaic of habitat types. Historical ecology information such as this can be used to create contemporary habitat zones that guide urban biodiversity actions that can work together to restore some of the habitat diversity that has been lost.

Source: Grossinger et al. 2006 and 2008, Beller et al. 2010

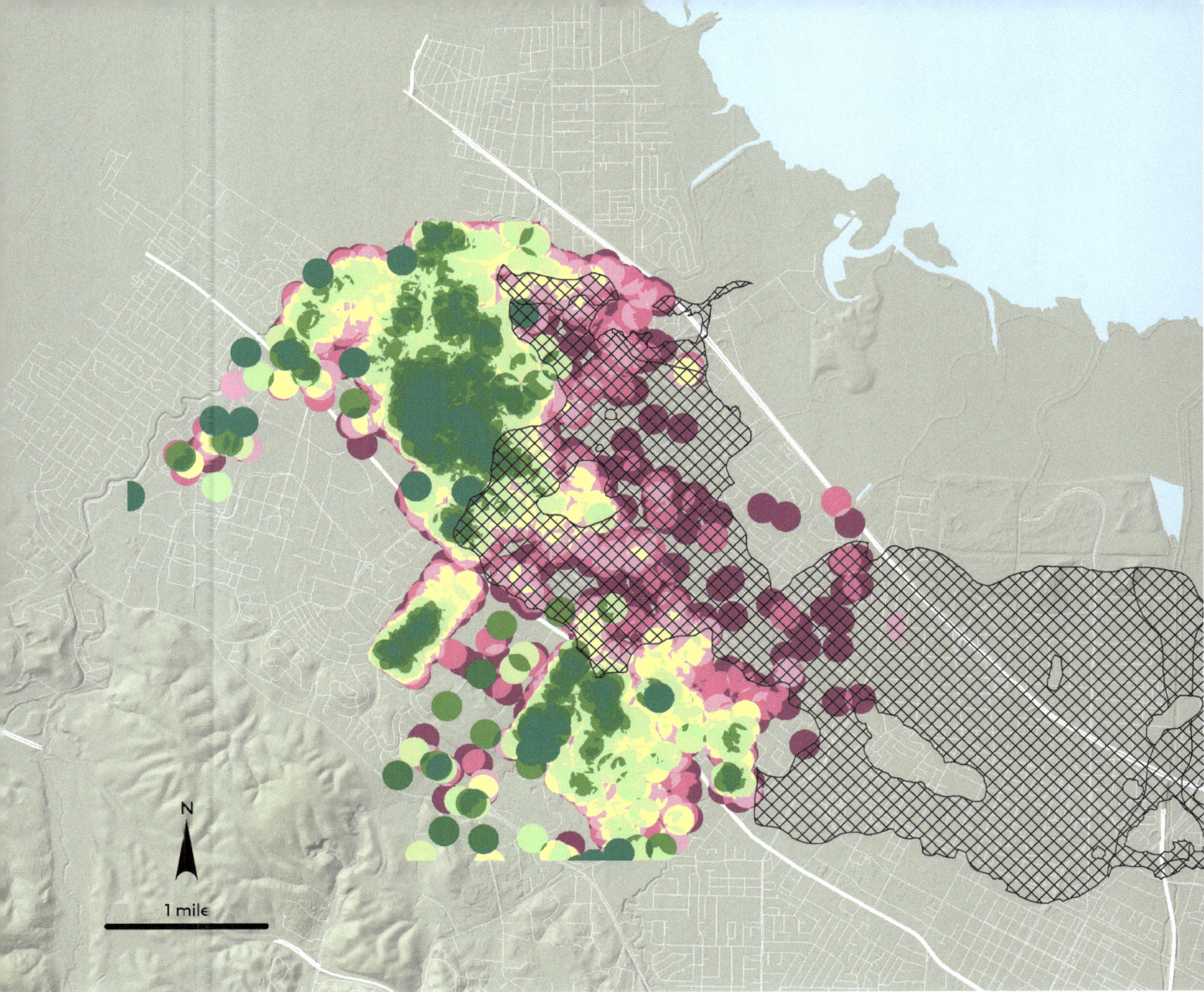

Palo Alto Oaks and Historical Wet Meadow

⬚⬚⬚⬚ Historical Wet Meadow

Oaks within 500 foot radius of each surveyed tree

- ○ 0
- 0.1 – 2.6
- 2.7 – 5.2
- 5.3 – 10.4
- 10.5 – 16.8
- 16.9 – 24.6
- 24.7 – 34.9
- 35 – 47.9
- 48 – 72.5
- 72.6 – 330

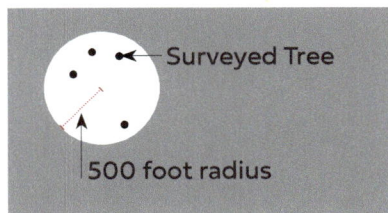

Surveyed Tree

500 foot radius

Figure 3.13 The city of *Palo Alto* has preserved many of its oaks. A comprehensive survey of all the native oaks in the city reveals a striking pattern of persistence: native oaks remain abundant in former oak woodlands, occurring at lower densities where seasonal wet meadows were historically present. This boundary tracks today, as historically, the divide between heavier clay-rich soils along the Bay and loamier soils on high ground. The density of oaks in Palo Alto today, between 2 and 12 trees per hectare, is similar to that of historical valley oak woodlands in Silicon Valley (Grossinger et al. 2008). These trees are now integrated into the urban landscape, and are surrounded by other non-native trees, lawns, buildings and roads. Oaks in Palo Alto provide an example of how the spatial distribution of a foundation tree species characteristic of a particular habitat type can be preserved and recreated in an urban setting. Accompanying understory vegetation alongside oaks could help to mimic the spatial attributes of oak woodland habitat types more effectively.

ARBOREAL SALAMANDER

The arboreal salamander (*Aneides lugubris*) is common throughout California's coast ranges. Tolerant of urbanization, arboreal salamanders can be found in yards and parks throughout Silicon Valley where oaks are present. They are found most commonly in oak woodland habitats, and are an example of a species that would benefit from the creation of coherent patches of oak woodland habitat in the urban landscape.

Arboreal salamanders move between habitat on the ground and in trees. During the wet season, they can be found in leaf litter, tree bark, rotting logs, or tree cavities, emerging at night to forage. They are adept climbers and have been recorded in tree cavities sixty feet above the ground. During the dry season, salamanders retreat to moist locations, such as rodent burrows, caves, tree cavities, wells, or water tanks. Females lay their eggs in these dry season refuges, caring for them until they hatch in autumn. While the species is generally solitary, many individuals may congregate in a single moist location during the dry season. Preserving or creating vertical complexity similar to what exists in oak woodlands can help support arboreal salamanders. Maintaining leaf litter, rodent burrows, and trees with cavities, may also increase foraging and estivation habitat.

(Sources: Zeiner et al. 1988, Bartholomew 2000, Parra-Olea et al. 2008)

(Photo courtesy of Greg Schechter, CC by 2.0)

DIET: Insects including beetles, ants, caterpillars, and centipedes, and possibly fungi.

HABITAT: Arboreal salamanders occur primarily in oak woodlands in California's Coast Range and the Sierra Nevada foothills, though they can also be found in douglas fir (*Pseudotsugo menziesii*) and redwood (*Sequoia sempervirens*) forests in the region. The species requires moist crevices for estivation.

HOME RANGE: Likely under 1 acre.

KEY STRESSORS: The primary threat to the species is loss of large oaks in which it nests and estivates. Predation may also impact the salamander's numbers.

Figure 3.14 *The arboreal salamander has a small home range. Dependent on oak woodland habitats, salamanders can be found in the urban landscape where native oaks are present. Preserving and restoring these historical habitat types benefits species that have co-evolved with these plant communities.*

ELEMENT 05: NATIVE VEGETATION

The Silicon Valley landscape is dominated by non-native vegetation and trees. Riparian corridors along Coyote Creek and Guadalupe River and larger urban parks contain mostly native riparian and oak trees (Fig 3.15). However, outside these areas, the majority of the urban forest is made up of several hundred non-native trees, and lawns and ornamental species form the dominant understory vegetation in most areas outside parks.

The relative rarity of native trees across Silicon Valley is likely a barrier for native wildlife that has adapted to the specific conditions and resources that these trees provide. Numerous native insects, such as *Cynipid* wasps and California sister butterflies (*Adelpha californica*), rely upon specific native plant species as host plants for their young. Where these plants are absent, associated wildlife will likely also be rare or absent, which can have impacts that cascade through the food chain (Heleno et al. 2009). Other animals with specific diets reliant upon native plants, such as the acorn woodpecker (*Melanerpes formicivorus*), may also be absent from parts of the urban environment where native oaks are not found (Koenig and Haydock 1999). Non-native plants may alter soil chemistry with potential impacts on soil microbial communities and the biodiversity they support (Batten et al. 2006). Some ornamental plants, such as glossy privets (*Ligustrum lucidum*), may become invasive and outcompete native plants outside of landscaped areas (Wolf and DiTomaso 2016). These species have the potential to further diminish habitat for animals dependent on native plants.

While it is clear that the majority of vegetation in the Silicon Valley landscape is non-native, quantifying native vegetation cover is a challenge with currently available datasets. Over the last decade, several cities in Silicon Valley have created publicly-available inventories of all municipally owned trees, including trees along streets, in public parks, in schools, and along transportation rights-of-way. While these inventories do not include trees on private property, they show the proportion of municipally owned trees that are native. In Palo Alto, the local urban forestry nonprofit Canopy has also conducted a comprehensive survey of all native oak trees in the city, including on private property. This dataset provides a unique window into the total number, density, and spatial distribution of trees that are foundational in oak ecosystems of California. In addition, SCVWD, a local flood control agency, has identified native and non-native canopy cover along Silicon Valley's waterways using field surveys as well as ground and aerial imagery classification. The publicly available statewide dataset CalVeg (USDA Forest

Service Vegetation Classification & Mapping, based on satellite imagery with field verification) identifies native and non-native habitats in protected areas. Taken together, these datasets paint a picture of the total abundance and distribution of native vegetation. Other urban areas may face similar data challenges, but planners can likely assume that exotic species dominate unprotected lands in many cities (Hitchmough 2011).

To support native fauna, property owners can select native plant species as they landscape and avoid planting or remove plant species that have the potential to become invasive in Silicon Valley. Native fauna will likely benefit most from assemblages of native vegetation that resemble the natural landscape.

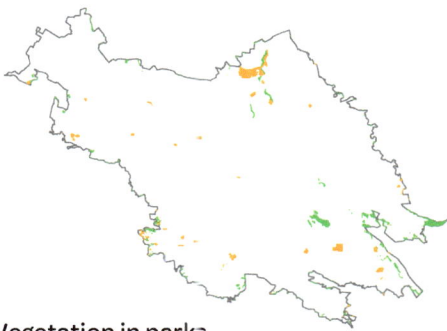

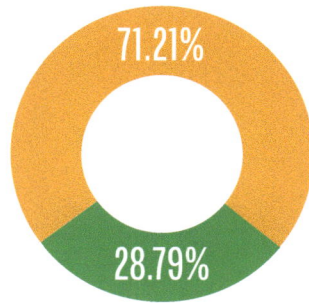

Vegetation in parks
SOURCE: CalVeg

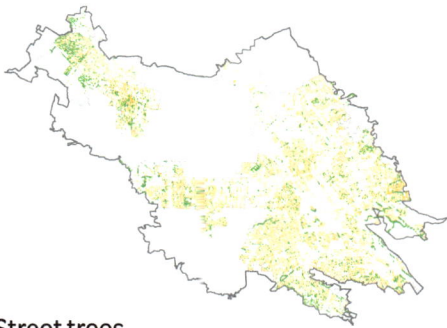

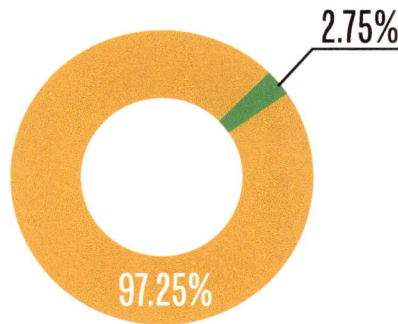

Street trees
SOURCE: City Street Tree Inventories

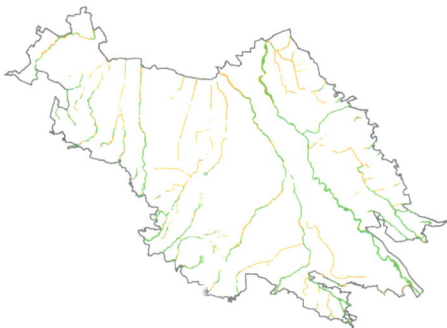

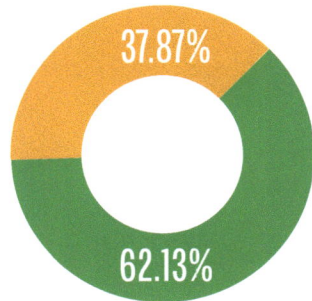

Vegetation along stream corridors
SOURCE: SCVWD

Non-Native Vegetation

Native Vegetation

Figure 3.15 The proportion of native vegetation within parks, among street trees, and along streams. The street tree map compares the number of individual native and non-native municipally owned trees, and does not include privately owned trees in residential properties. Data comes from street tree inventories from several cities (East Palo Alto, Palo Alto, Cupertino, Mountain View, and San Jose), from CalVeg, and from SCVWD riparian vegetation survey. See appendix for more details on all analyses.

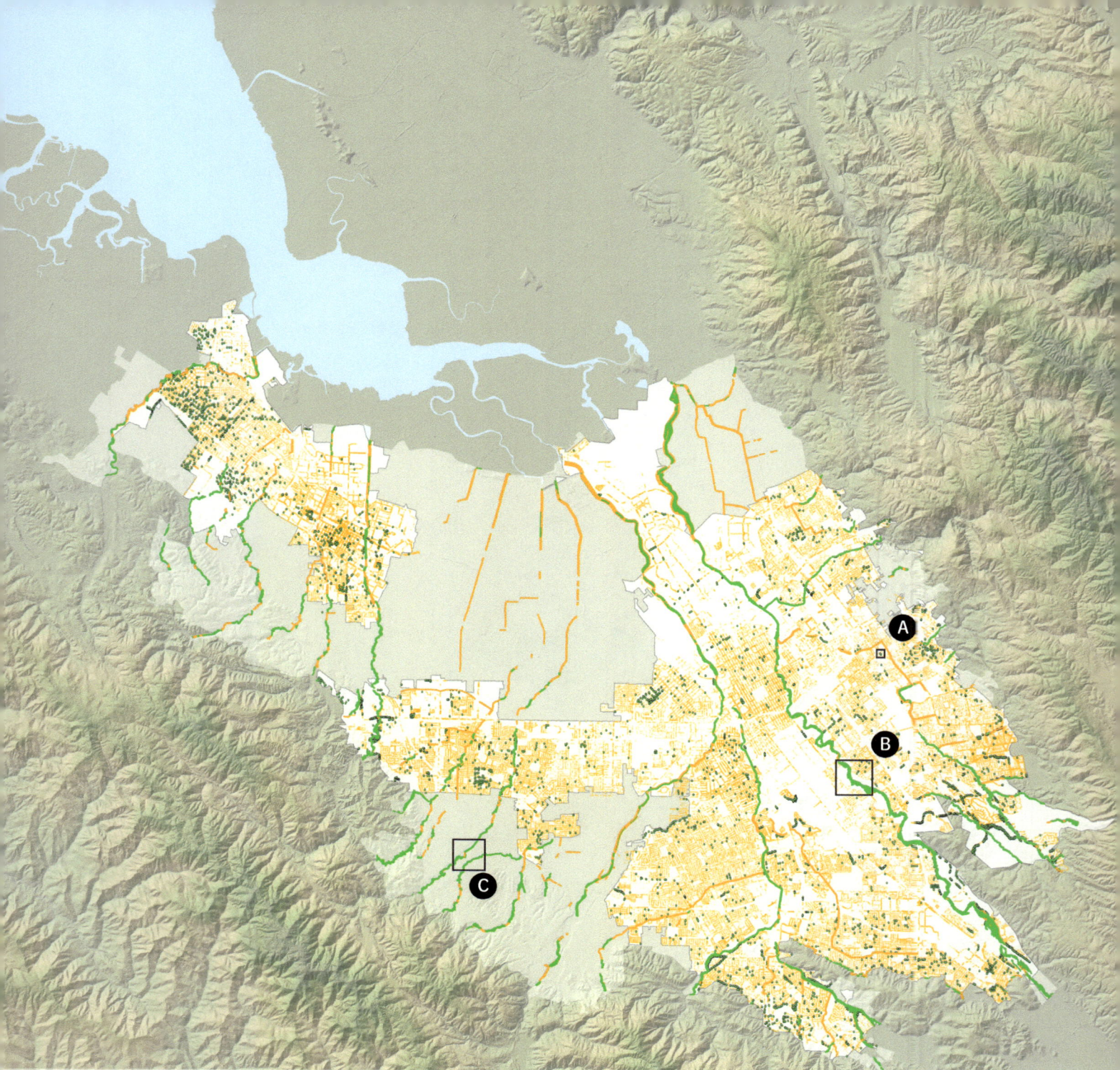

Silicon Valley **Native Vegetation**

N

5 miles

- 🟩 **Native Habitat (CalVeg)**
- 🟧 **Non-Native Habitat (CalVeg)**
- **Native Stream Vegetation (SCVWD)**
- **Non-Native Stream Vegetation (SCVWD)**
- **Native Street Trees (street tree inventory data)**
- **Non-Native Street Trees (street tree inventory data)**

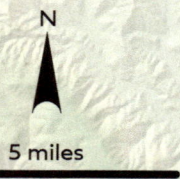

Figure 3.16 The distribution of native and non-native vegetation in municipally-owned street trees (based on street tree inventory data), stream vegetation (based on SCVWD data), and habitat types in parks (based on CalVeg data). These datasets have varying levels of spatial resolution; see appendix for more details.

A. Non-native trees. Kollmar Drive is a neighborhood in San Jose with mixed land use, including single-family homes, apartments, and commercial buildings. This area contains a mixture of native and non-native trees, as well as areas with canopy gaps where native trees could be planted. The green dots in the center of the frame represent a grove of native California sycamores (*Platanus racemosa*), while the surrounding orange dots represent non-native trees. Additional native street trees could be installed in the parking lots, many of which lack trees.

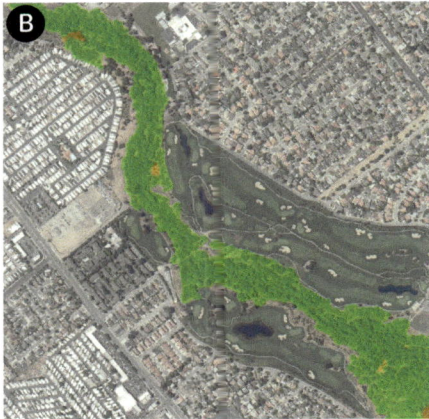

B. Riparian forests. Coyote Creek near Los Lagos Golf Course is an example of predominantly native riparian vegetation. The stream corridor is up to 300 feet wide in some areas. SCVWD riparian survey data identifies this area as containing mostly native riparian vegetation, including a mix of coast live oak (*Quercus agrifolia*), valley oak (*Quercus lobata*), elderberry (*Sambucus nigra*), red willow (*Salix laevigata*) and California sycamore.

C. Agricultural park. Heritage Orchard, a protected area in Saratoga, is a demonstration farm that showcases the region's agricultural history. The orchard's stonefruit trees are mostly non-native, but hold cultural and educational value. Park managers can improve the orchard's support for biodiversity by planting native wildflowers or other indigenous vegetation along the park's perimeter, and integrating native trees alongside stonefruit. These interventions could improve the orchard's agricultural yield by supporting local pollinators.

MONARCH BUTTERFLY

The Monarch butterfly (*Danaus plexippus*) is found throughout the United States and is relatively tolerant of urbanization. Populations have been steadily declining in western North America over the past twenty years (Jepsen et al. 2015). Various factors have contributed to the species' decline, including increasingly frequent drought conditions, parasites, and a loss of milkweed, the species' host plant. Butterflies lay their eggs and monarch caterpillars feed upon a variety of species within the milkweed subfamily, including both native and non-native plants.

Tropical milkweed (*Asclepias curassavica*), a non-native species commonly cultivated in California, grows year-round, whereas native milkweed species die back in the winter. Tropical milkweed's growth pattern disrupts seasonal cues for monarchs that use it, and may increase the risk of pathogen transmission (Satterfield et al. 2016). Growing native milkweed species, such as narrowleaf milkweed (*Asclepias fascicularis*), can help augment monarch habitat in Silicon Valley.

(Source: Jepsen et al. 2015, USFS n.d.)

DIET: Monarch caterpillars feed exclusively on leaves from milkweeds (subfamily Asclepiadoideae). Adult butterflies consume nectar from a variety of flowers.

HABITAT: Monarchs require milkweed plants on which to lay their eggs and to sustain caterpillars. Adult monarchs require flowering plants for nectar and groves of trees along the coast (especially stands of conifers and eucalyptus) for overwintering.

HOME RANGE: Monarchs are highly migratory. In western North America, monarchs overwinter in dense groups along the California coast. In the spring, they disperse north as far as Washington and west as far as Arizona.

KEY STRESSORS: Maintaining sufficient Milkweed habitat is critical for Monarch populations. Parasites and pathogens, pesticide use, climate change, and logging in wintering habitat are all additional stressors for monarchs.

Figure 3.17 The monarch butterfly depends on the availability of native milkweed plants along its migratory corridors. Planting native milkweed in urban landscapes along migratory routes can help sustain Monarch populations.

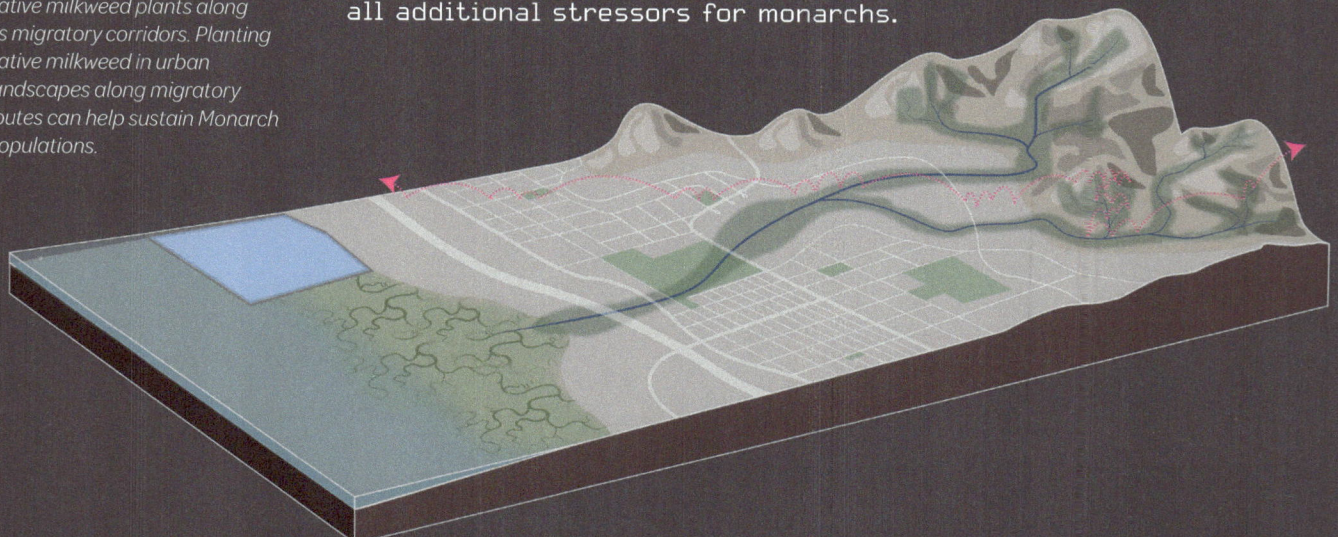

(Photo courtesy of Oakley, CC by 2.0)

(Photo courtesy of Erica Fleniken, CC by 2.0)

As is true across ecosystems globally, species native to Silicon Valley rely on specific components of the landscape such as large trees, water, and other physical structures to complete their life cycles. In California, water is often a limiting resource for native flora and fauna. Silicon Valley's ponds, lakes, streams, and rivers hold water through much or all of the year, permitting many species to survive. Thus, local water bodies provide home to a diversity of aquatic insects, amphibians, and fish, as well as birds, mammals, and other terrestrial animals (Howard et al. 2013). Many wetlands have been removed or altered during development, and urban streams are also highly modified. In many urban water bodies, contaminants have impacted ecosystem health (Grossinger et al. 2006, Grossinger et al. 2008, Beller et al. 2010). Water quality monitoring, pollution reduction, and aquatic habitat restoration efforts are underway throughout the valley to address these issues (e.g., Santa Clara Valley Urban Runoff Pollution Prevention Program, South Bay Salt Pond Restoration Project). Continued action to protect aquatic ecosystems stands to benefit the diverse set of species dependent on Silicon Valley's limited water resources.

Large trees also provide special resources for a diversity of organisms. In Silicon Valley, large oak trees were common in the oak woodlands that dominated the historical landscape. Many native species are adapted to use large native oaks to meet their ecological needs. Acorn woodpeckers consume acorns from valley, coast live, black, and other oak species, and store acorns in the bark of large trees (>32 inches in diameter at breast height). Many woodpecker species also excavate cavities in large trees, creating nesting habitat for themselves and other birds. Large oak trees also support diverse insect communities, including many species that are highly specialized to consume oak leaves and lay their eggs in oak branches. Reptiles and small mammals take refuge in downed woody debris from large native oak trees. Today, large native oaks are relatively rare in Silicon Valley. While some species have transitioned to using non-native trees to meet their needs, others, particularly oak specialists, have dwindled in this novel ecosystem. Efforts to "re-oak" Silicon Valley by planting new groves of native oaks and preserving extant large oaks could help oak-dependent species survive in the urban environment (Spotswood et al. 2017).

Opportunities to preserve and protect special resources are present across the urban landscape. Re-oaking initiatives can aim to integrate oaks along streets, in private yards, and on commercial properties. Where large water features are lacking in dense urban areas, small features such as bird baths and fountains can be beneficial. The urban environment lacks many features that historically provided shelter for native species. In their place, some man-made structures may serve as adequate substitutes. Nest boxes may benefit cavity-nesting birds, such as western bluebirds (*Sialia mexicana*) and chestnut-backed chickadees (*Poecile rufescens*). Because non-native species may also benefit from nest boxes, careful design and placement are important to limit negative impacts Analogous to nest boxes for birds, "bee hotels" may provide nesting habitat for native solitary bees, including the black-tailed bumble bee. Meanwhile, piles of woody debris and leaf litter may benefit insects, reptiles, and amphibians that typically take refuge within decaying organic matter (Hagan and Grove 1999).

We used Silicon Valley wetland mapping and street tree inventories to quantify the availability of special resource in the region. In other cities in the United States, the National Wetlands Inventory may provide geospatial data for wetlands. Where detailed tree maps are not available, satellite imagery or LiDAR may provide insight into the locations of large trees. Cities that protect heritage trees may also collect data on their locations.

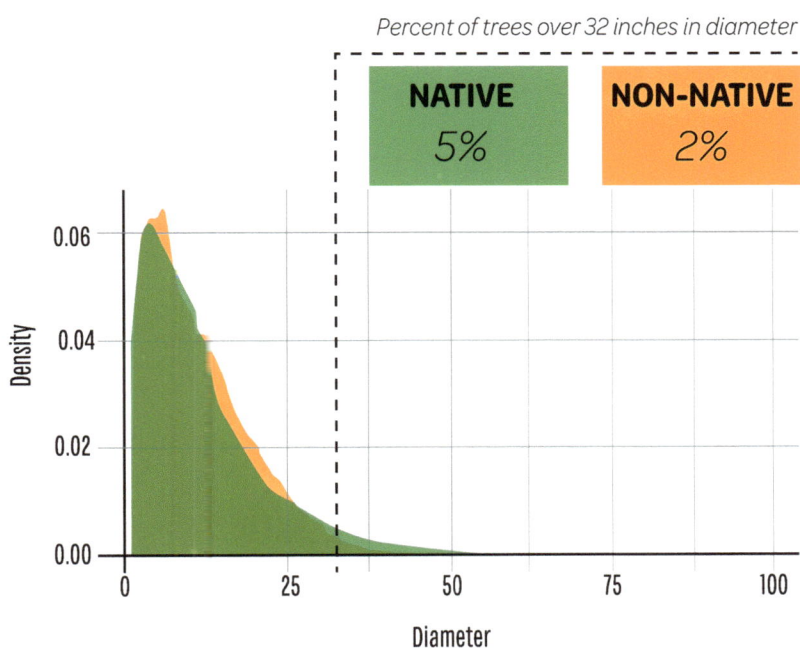

Figure 3.18 Large trees are relatively rare on the landscape, and represent a similar fraction of both native and non-native trees. Data are taken from street tree inventories from the cities of Mountain View, Cupertino, and San Jose. The large tree threshold is based on the average size of granary trees used by acorn woodpeckers (Gutierrez and Koenig 1978). See appendix for more details.

Status	Size	Trees	Percent
Native	large	391	5
Native	small	6,963	94
Non-Native	large	4398	2
Non-Native	small	200,941	98

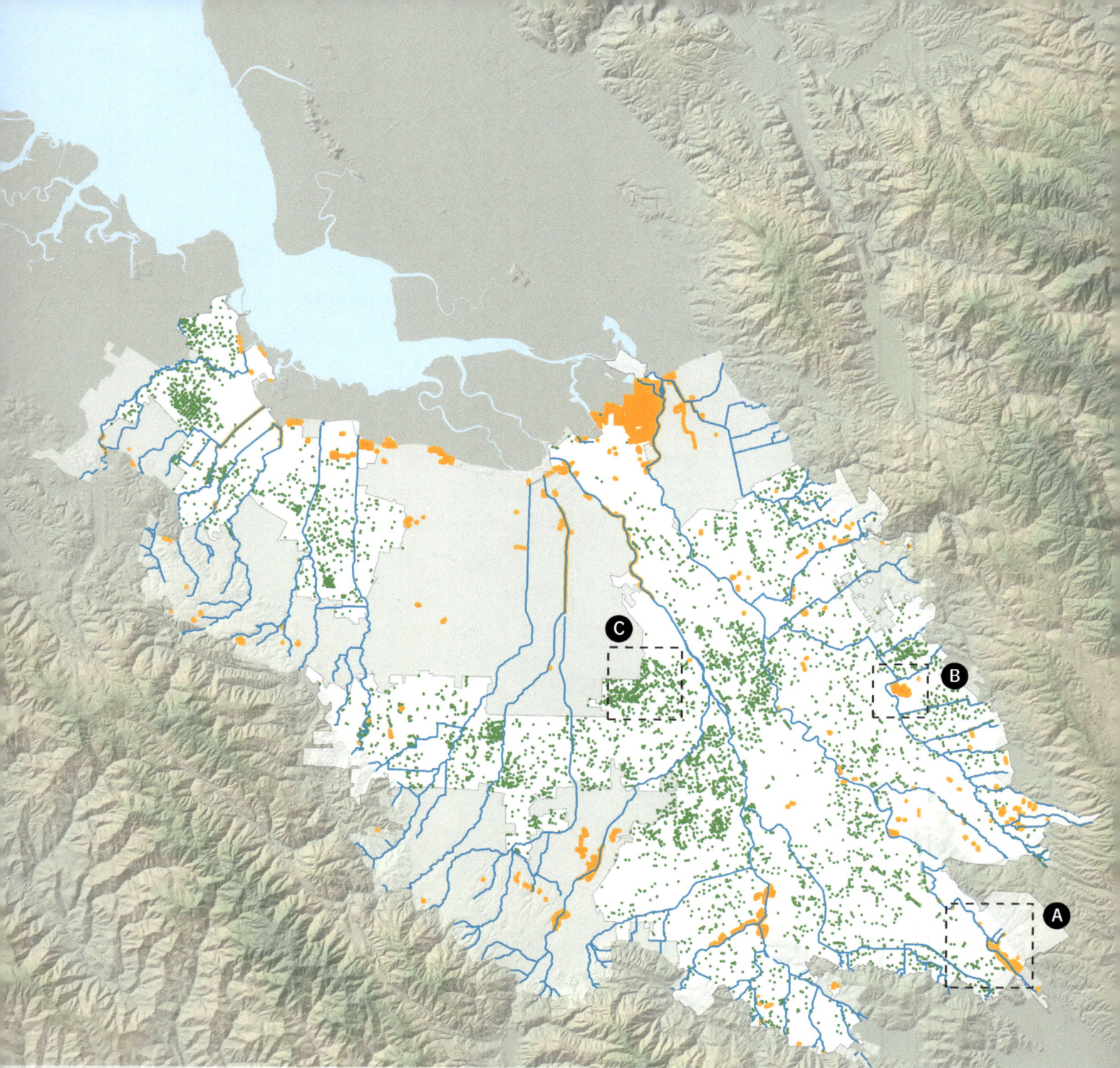

Silicon Valley Special Resources:
Large Trees and Aquatic Resources

N

5 miles

— Stream

▬ Wetland

Large street trees (>32 inches in diameter)

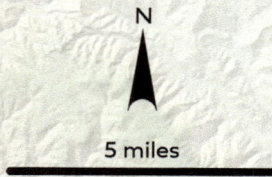

Figure 3.19 The distribution of special resources in the region, including large trees, wetlands, and streams. Large trees (>32 inches in diameter) are taken from street tree inventory data from several cities. Wetland habitat types and streams are identified using the Bay Area Aquatic Resources Inventory. See appendix for more details.

A. Large valley oaks at risk. The Santa Teresa neighborhood of San Jose is a dense housing development with few large trees. At the center of the neighborhood, an undeveloped 16-acre lot contains two massive (>50 inches in diameter) valley oaks on its periphery. Birds commonly found in oak woodlands such as oak titmice, white-breasted nuthatch, and nuttall's woodpeckers have all been found nearby (eBird, 2019). San Jose has designated the trees as "heritage oaks," though recent development plans for the parcel may place the trees at risk of removal. Mountain View, Palo Alto, Sunnyvale, and other cities in Silicon Valley have similar tree protections that increase the chances large trees will continue to provide habitat for the Silicon Valley ecosystem into the future.

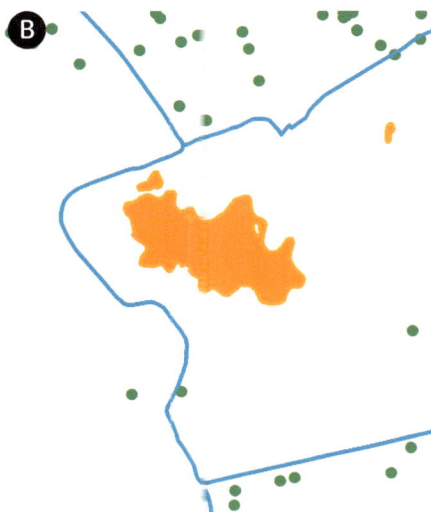

(Photo by Erica Spotswood)

B. Large lake. Lake Cunningham Park in San Jose is a 200-acre park adjacent to Thompson Creek that boasts some of the highest bird diversity in Silicon Valley. The artificial lake and its surrounding wetlands are some of the largest remaining tracts of wetland in the region, and the park attracts many aquatic species, such as white pelicans and ruddy ducks, as well as species that visit the wetlands in search of food and water, such as bobcats and raccoons (iNaturalist 2019). The park's aquatic resources, close vicinity to urban areas, and large size likely allow it to act as a regional biodiversity hub where both urban-tolerant and urban-avoiding species can thrive.

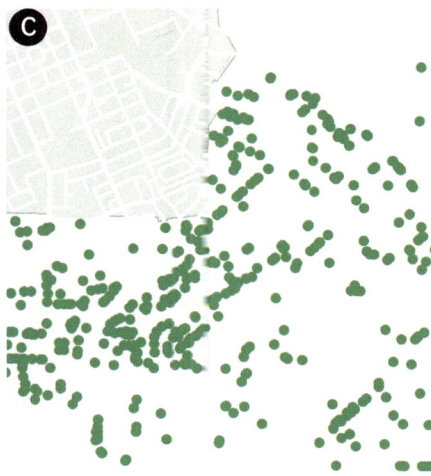

(Photo courtesy of Don DeBold, CC by 2.0)

C. Old neighborhood with large trees. The Rose Garden district of San Jose is one of the city's oldest residential neighborhoods, with some homes dating back to the 19th century (USGS 1899). The neighborhood has one of the highest concentrations of large trees in Silicon Valley. These trees provide habitat for a diversity of native animals, from Anna's hummingbirds to ground squirrels to black-tailed bumblebees (eBird 2019, iNaturalist 2019). Approximately half of the large street trees are native oaks, while the remainder are predominantly exotic ornamental species. Rose Garden residents can augment the area's habitat value by increasing native canopy cover, planting native understory plants, and supporting the protection of existing large trees.

(Photo courtesy of Google Earth, 2019)

ACORN WOODPECKER

Acorn woodpeckers (*Melanerpes formicivorus*) live in colonies of 2-15 birds that together defend 4 to 22 acre territories. Acorns from oaks native to California (including coast live oak and valley oak) are a critical food source for the species. In the fall, colonies stock acorns in granaries – large, living or dead trees where woodpeckers drill holes for acorn storage. Adults consume stored acorns from the winter through the spring, then broaden their diets to include more insects, fruit, and other food items.

Acorn woodpeckers are tolerant of urbanization, and are found in some cities in Silicon Valley where oak trees are common (Rottenborn 1999, eBird 2019). Large trees (>32 inches in diameter) that can be used for granaries are often a limiting resource (Koenig et al. 1999), and conserving these special resources along with native oak trees may enable Silicon Valley to better support the species. Oak groves that contain at least twenty trees, including potential granaries, and cover 15-20 acres have the potential to support new colonies of Acorn woodpeckers [see "Re-oaking Silicon Valley", Spotswood et al. 2017].

(Source: Zeiner et al. 1988)

(Photo courtesy of Tim Dickey, CC by 2.0)

DIET: Acorns, flying insects, sap, as well as oak catkins and flower nectar. Needs daily water.

HABITAT: Open oak woodlands and mixed oak-conifer forests.

HOME RANGE: Territories of colonies range from 4 to 22 acres in size, with an average of 17 acres, typically including at least one large tree used as a granary (Koenig et al. 1995).

KEY STRESSORS: Acorn crop production, availability of large trees for cavity nesting and granaries, competition and nestling predation.

(Photo courtesy of Tim Dickey, CC by 2.0)

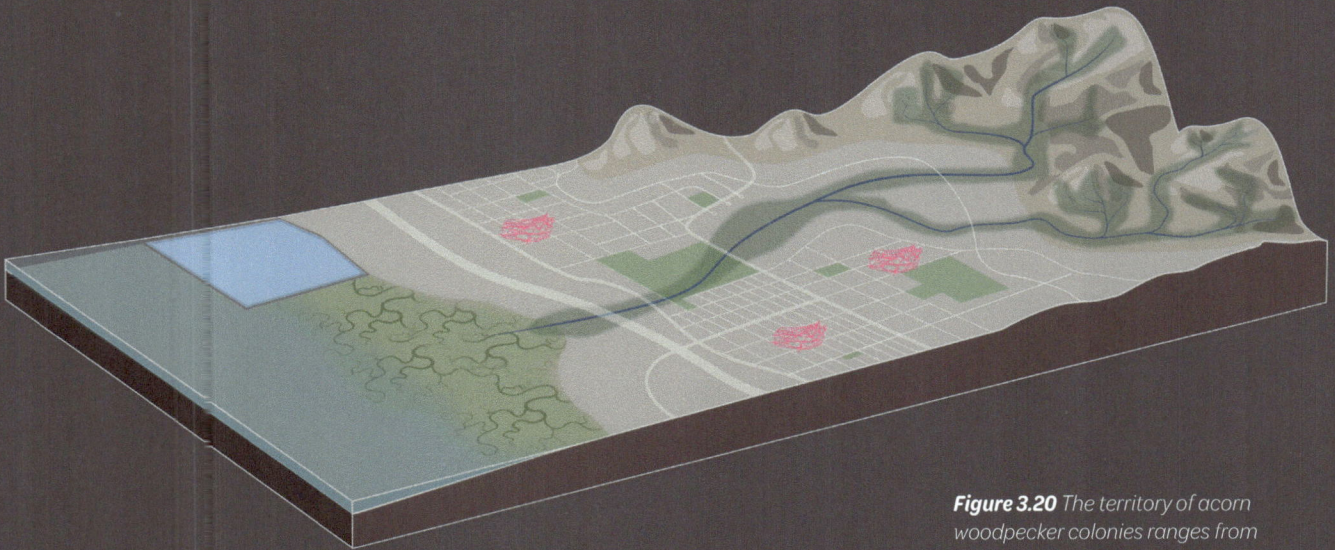

Figure 3.20 *The territory of acorn woodpecker colonies ranges from 4-22 acres in size. They depend on the availability of large trees and native oaks in their home range for acorn storage and nesting, and will use the urban landscape if these key resources are available.*

ELEMENT 07: MANAGEMENT

The urban landscape of Silicon Valley is a patchwork of ownership and land use types. This variety results in highly variable type, frequency and intensity of management with varying degrees of impact on biodiversity. Data that quantifies and describes these interventions is not readily available for areas outside protected open spaces. We have chosen, therefore, to highlight how interventions can be timed to match California's unique Mediterranean climate. Management informed by the seasonality of key ecological and physical processes can minimize impacts to biodiversity. This type of seasonal schedule could be re-created in any city following the local climate and timing of ecological processes.

The following diagram describes how management actions can be timed to best support biodiversity in Silicon Valley. This list is not exhaustive, and there are other types of management that are not temporally specific that can also be beneficial, such as decompacting soil and modifying traffic patterns (See Management in Chapter 2 for more detail). While seasonal schedules provide useful guidance for current conditions, they can vary from year to year, and are expected to shift with a changing climate.

(Photo courtesy of USDA, CC by 2.0)

(Photo courtesy Don DeBold, CC by 2.0)

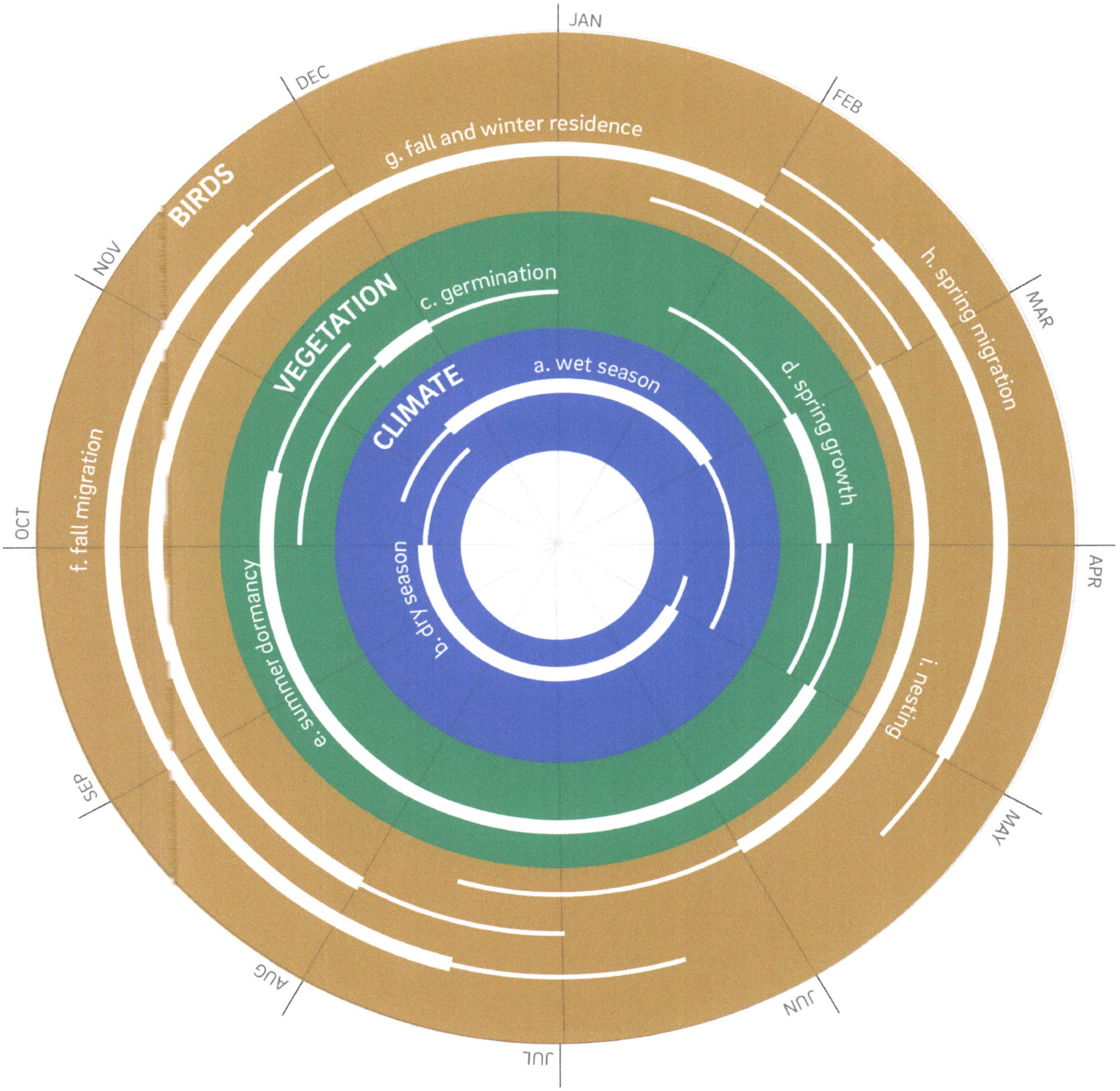
JAN
FEB
MAR
APR
MAY
JUN
JUL
AUG
SEP
OCT
NOV
DEC
BIRDS
g. fall and winter residence
h. spring migration
i. nesting
f. fall migration
VEGETATION
c. germination
d. spring growth
e. summer dormancy
CLIMATE
a. wet season
b. dry season

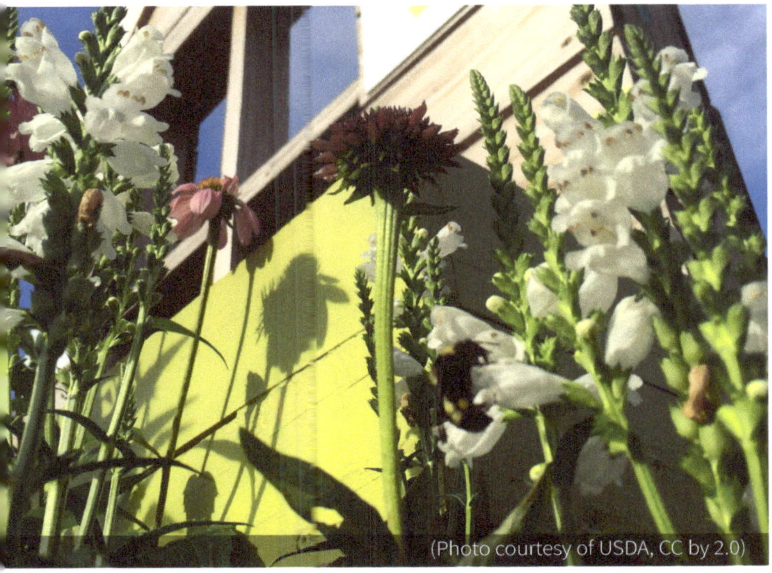
(Photo courtesy of USDA, CC by 2.0)

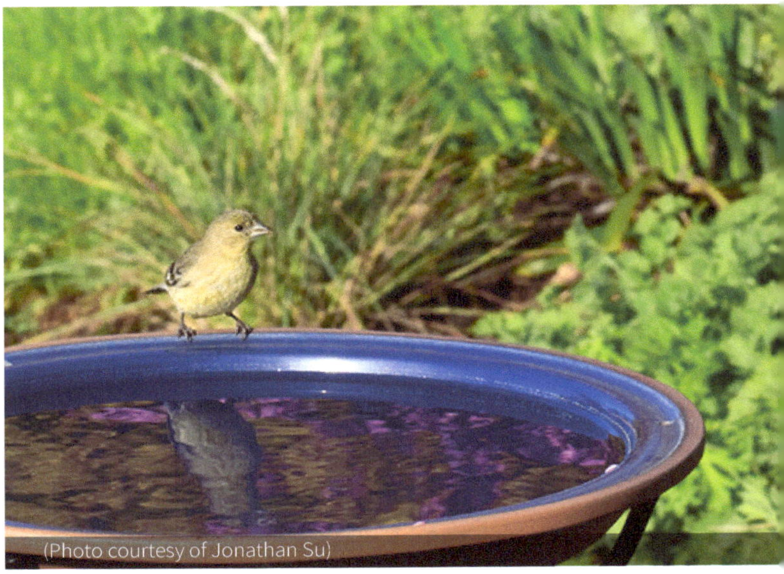
(Photo courtesy of Jonathan Su)

Biodiversity management for Silicon Valley following climate, growing, and migration seasons

(Photo courtesy Don DeBold, CC by 2.0)

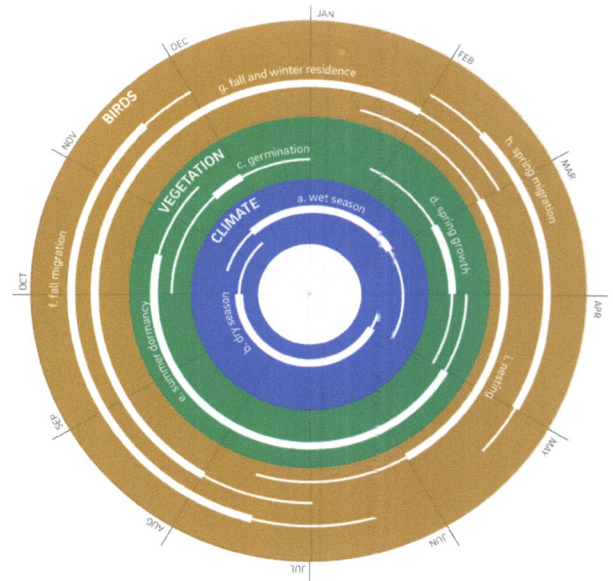

Wheel		Time	Definition	Management Action
CLIMATE	A	Wet season (mid-October - May)	First rains in the region typically arrive between October and November, continuing intermittently until around May.	Reducing pesticide use during the wet season can limit runoff into sensitive aquatic habitat types.
	B	Dry season (May - mid-October)	Little rain typically falls between late May and early October.	Many drought-tolerant native plants are sensitive to summer water, and irrigation can be eliminated during the dry season once plants are established. Lawn removal during the dry season will provide time for the establishment of native plants in winter and early spring.
GROWING SEASONS	C	Germination (mid-October - February)	With the first rains of the season, seeds from annual grasses and forbs germinate, turning the landscape green. Perennial plants sprout new growth above- and below-ground. Many native California trees, such as Valley Oaks, drop their leaves in the rainy season and winter.	During or prior to this season, sites should be prepared for planting by clearing undesirable vegetation, decompacting soils, or other soil health amendments. Perennial invasive plants can be treated or cleared in ecologically valuable areas ahead of flower and seeding stages. Allowing leaf litter to remain on the ground will provide habitat for overwintering insects, and will create mulch that improves soil health ahead of spring growth.
	D	Spring growth (March - May)	Warmer temperatures and longer days promote vigorous growth in annual plants, followed quickly by flowering and seed production as soils begin to dry out. Most perennial plants continue to grow, flower and set seed toward the end of the primary growing season in May.	During this time, invasive annual grasses such as wild oat (*Avena fatua*) grow aggressively, as well as some perennial plants such as English ivy (*Hedera Helix*), giant reed (*Arundo durax*) and French broom (*Genista monspessulana*). Removal of these plants before they set seed can help reduce competition with native plants. Invasive Mediterranean annual grasses aggressively colonize vacant spaces in urban areas, and management to reduce these species is necessary to maintain native plants in urban settings.

Wheel		Time	Definition	Management Actions
GROWING SEASONS	E	Summer dormancy (June - mid-October)	Many annual plants die and deposit seeds that lie dormant in the soil until the next rainy season. Above ground, many perennial plants go dormant, though underground roots and stem crowns remain. Some trees and shrubs, such as coast live oak and toyon (*Heteromeles arbutifolia*) retain most of their leaves during the summer. Some native plants bloom in the summer or early fall, including some tarweeds (*Madia spp.*) and sunflowers (e.g., *Helianthus spp.*).	Several non-native invasive plants such as Himalayan blackberry (*Rubus armeniacus*) and fennel (*Foeniculum vulgare*) set seed later in the summer or fall. Removal and control of these plants before they set seed can help reduce competition with native plants.
MIGRATION and NESTING*	F	Avian Fall Migration (mid-August - November)	Many birds (including many seabirds, shorebirds, raptors, waterfowl and land birds) and some insects (including many dragonflies, beetles, butterflies, and moths) embark on long journeys at this time of year. Summer residents leave to return to their wintering grounds, while winter residents migrate south to this region to overwinter.	During migration periods, management of nighttime light is an important component of bird-safe urban design. Using wildlife-friendly exterior lighting and reducing interior building lights can help reduce potential for birds and insects to lose their way or collide with windows. Providing seeds and planting native plants that produce berries in the fall can also help birds build fat during stopovers or before migration.
	G	Overwintering period (December - mid-February)	Many raptors, shorebirds, and waterbirds spend the wet winter months in our landscape before returning to their summer breeding grounds. Some migratory insects also overwinter, many relying on ground litter for shelter. A limited number of residents, such as Anna's Hummingbird (*Calypte anna*), nest during this time.	Establishing bird feeders can benefit birds that overwinter locally. Maintaining leaf litter on the ground can help support insect populations during the winter, which are an important food source for many overwintering birds. Planting native plants that flower in the winter can provide nectar sources for hummingbirds (e.g., Anna's hummingbirds) that overwinter in the region. Similarly, planting native plants that produce berries in the winter such as madrone and toyon can provide food for wintering species such as thrushes and waxwings.
	H	Spring Migration (mid-February - May)	Summer residents migrate north to this region for the summer, while winter residents leave the area to return northward.	As in fall migration, managing nighttime light is important for migrating birds in the spring. Erecting bird boxes before nesting season will allow birds to become familiar with nesting opportunities before the breeding season begins.
	I	Summer residence / avian nesting season (March - August)	During this ecologically sensitive time, many migratory and resident birds in the area begin the breeding season.	Reducing mowing and pruning can reduce the risk of harming birds during the breeding season. Providing water through fountains and bird baths can help support more birds during the dry season. Providing bird boxes, and where possible, retaining dying trees and branches, can help support birds that nest in cavities. Keeping cats indoors and managing feral cats can reduce predation on eggs and nestlings. Planting native plants that produce berries in the summer, such as elderberry (*Sambucus spp.*) can provide food for birds during the postbreeding period as they build fat to prepare for fall migration.

*Not all birds and insects migrate. Many resident birds and insects live in this region year round.
Migration periods in this table represent typical patterns, although exact timing varies depending on the species and the year.

BLACK CROWNED NIGHT HERON

Black-crowned night-herons (*Nycticorax nycticorax*) frequent the ponds, streams and other wetlands of Silicon Valley. The stout birds primarily forage nocturnally and rest in dense foliage during the day. From February through July, they congregate to form nesting colonies in trees or marsh habitats. A single tree may support dozens of breeding heron pairs.

Black-crowned night herons can benefit from thoughtful management strategies. Frequent disturbance to nesting colonies may prevent breeding pairs from laying eggs, cause pairs to abandon their nests, and increase nestling mortality (Tremblay and Ellison 1979). For example, in 2014, arborists unintentionally knocked down heron nests and injured nestlings while trimming the branches of a nesting colony tree in downtown Oakland, California (Ortega-Welch 2018). The public outcry following this event, and subsequent designation of the heron as Oakland's official bird, highlight how important urban wildlife can be to the public. Timing tree trimming outside the breeding season can prevent these types of accidents from occurring.

Night herons are also sensitive to environmental contaminants, including PCBs, which are common in urban landscapes around San Francisco Bay (Hothem et al. 2010). Efforts to reduce contaminants in the Bay and in local waterways, such as through installation of green infrastructure, could benefit herons.

(Photo courtesy Don DeBold, CC by 2.0)

DIET: Varied diet of fish, aquatic insects, amphibians, and terrestrial animals such as reptiles and small mammals.

HABITAT: Herons roost in wetlands and trees with dense foliage, sometimes far from the nearest body of water.

HOME RANGE: During nesting season, individuals may forage up to 5 miles from the nesting area.

KEY STRESSORS: While the species is generally tolerant of urbanization, human disturbance, loss of wetlands, and loss of nesting trees have impacted its numbers.

(Source: Tremblay and Ellison 1979, Zeiner et al. 1988, Cornell Lab of Ornithology 2019)

(Photo courtesy Don DeBold, CC by 2.0)

Figure 3.21 *The Black-crowned night-heron forages in wetlands and along streams of Silicon Valley at night. During nesting season, they will form colonies within five miles of these wetland habitats, moving back and forth between wetlands and nest trees.*

URBAN
BIODIVERSITY
PLANNING

4

Introduction

As a city or region sets out to develop biodiversity goals and align its greening initiatives, a comprehensive spatial analysis that draws on data for each of the seven elements (described in Chapter 3) is a fundamental first step. This analysis can help to identify existing opportunities to enhance biodiversity at the site or neighborhood-scale and to prioritize interventions. Data can also help to identify interventions that address multiple elements, and are therefore most likely to enhance existing biodiversity support. Since no one entity can implement the range of actions necessary to create an urban biodiversity network, a landscape-scale strategy can help communities develop a shared vision for where important actions, such as acquiring land, protecting ecosystems, and creating new habitat, is likely to be most impactful.

At early stages in the planning process, biodiversity data can support a landscape analysis, showing where current biodiversity lies and where it is lacking. Collecting systematic biodiversity data can provide a benchmark to help measure the efficacy of biodiversity initiatives over time (Samara Group LLC, Nilon et al. 2017). Projects can also create 'designed experiments' where design facilitates data collection (Felson & Pickett 2005) and scientific learning. Collaborative partnerships between ecologists and urban designers can ensure that manipulative experiments are established with the necessary treatments and replication to meet scientific standards. Designing projects with data collection in mind can also promote learning and adaptation over time, where project learning can inform the design of future projects (Ahern 2013).

Increasingly, data collected by citizens, or 'citizen scientists', is providing new opportunities to understand baseline biodiversity conditions, even in locations where systematically collected biodiversity data are sparse. The growing popularity of citizen science mobile apps and websites such as iNaturalist and eBird are increasing public engagement, and the availability of biodiversity data in cities (Callaghan et al. 2017, Spear et al. 2018). While these websites can provide valuable insight into what species currently occur where, data collection methods have biases, such as non-randomness in the location and time of sampling and differences in observers, that pose challenges for systematic analysis and interpretation. While many of these challenges can be overcome, it often requires substantial expertise in ecology and statistics to rigorously analyze citizen science datasets.

Identifying opportunities and priorities at the city scale can inform planning at the site scale. For example, habitat zones can be designed around existing special resources and can be used to determine plant species that property owners should cultivate within each zone. Within patches of open space, identifying resources that already support substantial biodiversity (e.g., high-quality habitat areas, large trees, water features, and sources of within-patch connectivity) can guide where additional habitat development will be most effective. Open space managers can expand these local features by, for example, replacing lawns and parking areas with greenery.

Plans for biodiversity have the most potential to succeed when they address all aspects of the urban biodiversity framework, regardless of the plans' spatial scale. For example, the process of identifying existing patches and their size across a city might

ELEMENT	POTENTIAL USEFUL DATA TYPES	POTENTIAL SOURCES	EXAMPLES APPLIED IN SILICON VALLEY*
PATCHES	Protected areas (fee title and easement)	Local or state government environmental planning offices, USGS Protected Areas Database of the US, Open Streets map	California Protected Areas Database
	Private greenspaces	Building and zoning footprints from City/county GIS portals	California Conservation Easement Database
CONNECTIONS	Physical stream data	Local or state government planning offices, USGS, Global Land Cover Facility	Bay Area Aquatic Resources Inventory (BAARI)
	Riparian vegetation surveys	Local, state or federal vegetation survey data	Santa Clara Valley Water District (SCVWD) riparian survey data
	Protected area networks	See Patches	See Patches
MATRIX QUALITY	Tree canopy cover	National Land Cover Database	Canopy cover layer from CalFire
	Delineated individual tree and shrub canopy	Analyzed from LiDAR (EarthDefine), municipal/county street tree inventory data	Street tree data from several local cities
	Impervious surface cover	National Land Cover Database	
	Land use	Local, regional or state land use datasets (e.g., USGS)	Association of Bay Area Governments
	Vegetation biomass	Normalized Difference Vegetation Index (NDVI)	
HABITAT DIVERSITY	Vegetation mapping	Local, state or federal vegetation surveys	CalVeg, SCVWD riparian surveys
	Historical ecology	Historical maps, illustrations, texts, photos, land surveys	SFEI Historical Ecology publications
	Groundwater	State planning offices, USGS	
	Soil maps	National Resources Conservation Service	
	Ecoregion	US Environmental Protection Agency Ecoregions	
NATIVE VEGETATION	Vegetation mapping	Local, state or federal vegetation surveys; citizen science observations (iNaturalist)	CalVeg, SCVWD riparian surveys
	Street trees	Municipal/county street tree inventories	Street tree inventories from several local cities
SPECIAL RESOURCES	Streams and wetlands	Local planning offices, National Wetlands Inventory (NWI)	Bay Area Aquatic Resources Inventory (BAARI)
	Large trees	Municipal/county street tree inventories	Street tree inventories from several cities
MANAGEMENT	Ecoregion	US Environmental Protection Agency Ecoregions	
	Timing of plant growth cycles	Phenology projects, citizen science observation networks, local ecology	CalFlora, iNaturalist, local ecology experts
	Timing of bird migrations	Citizen science observation networks, local ecology	eBird, local ecology experts

*These datasets were used to produce the figures found in Chapter 3. For more information see Appendix A.

highlight the importance of a particularly large patch. Identifying priorities for the landscape around the patch could focus on how to make the patch larger (patch size), increase its connectivity to other patches (connections) and improve the matrix around the patch (matrix quality). Meanwhile, planning improvements within patches could focus on the other elements of the framework, such as using habitat zones to define habitat types, planting native vegetation according to these zones, cultivating and protecting special resources, and employing wildlife-friendly management practices. Taken together, these actions will work synergistically to enhance biodiversity support within patches, along corridors, and within the urban matrix.

Acquiring land to create new patches and corridors in the urban landscape is one of the most powerful mechanisms for supporting biodiversity. New protected areas adjacent to existing patches can enlarge the size of habitat and increase the amount and diversity of resources available to resident wildlife. Land acquisitions can likewise fill gaps in corridors and enhance local and regional habitat connectivity. Creating new parks, dedicating conservation easements, and other mechanisms can also add new local and regional biodiversity hubs.

Where land acquisition is not feasible, improving existing patches, corridors, and matrix quality can increase habitat quality. For example, lawns in parks can be replaced with native plant communities representing a particular habitat zone. Cities can adopt wildlife-friendly management practices across their jurisdictions, plant local tree species along streets, and remove invasive species from stream corridors. These strategic enhancements can increase the effective size of patches and corridors, can increase connectivity by helping to fill gaps in corridors, and can act as virtual patches by creating habitat complexes in places outside of protected areas.

Changing trends in urban planning, land use, and redevelopment can also create opportunities to expand patches and fill gaps. Sprawling development patterns in the twentieth century may be replaced in the future by denser development (Warren et al. 2010). Increasing urban density may help protect existing biodiversity outside cities by preventing sprawl and, if densification preserves nature, could also create an opportunity to augment biodiversity support within the urban boundary (McKinney 2008).

Moving towards implementation

Planning and implementing urban biodiversity improvements will require broad-based public support. Biodiversity planning necessitates engaging with a variety of stakeholders, and public support for biodiversity improvements is key to their success. Communities long underrepresented in planning processes should have a significant role at the table, and mapping the geographic distribution of existing assets at a large scale can serve as a tool for a community participation process, guiding discussions about potential opportunity areas.

Moving from gathering data and analyzing the landscape towards implementing urban biodiversity actions can take many forms, and there is no single process that will apply to all cities. Biodiversity efforts are also not likely to follow a linear trajectory; successful biodiversity planning will be most effective if implemented through a variety of pathways both top-down and bottom-up. Yet alignment between efforts is essential to create the larger, connected, complex networks of urban nature that will provide the diverse functions needed as cities face growing challenges in the future.

Given the variety of land uses and stakeholders, there are many ways of achieving urban biodiversity goals. Some goals can be achieved through city-led actions within their jurisdictions. For example, cities can acquire parcels to create new parks, and can lead biodiversity planning within existing park systems. Other goals can be achieved by aligning biodiversity goals with planning and policy pathways. For example, biodiversity goals can be incorporated into plans for climate adaptation and water quality improvement. Some activities may require public outreach. For example, city-led planning can include public education to help homeowners interested in gardening for nature. Incentives, such as lawn conversion programs in water-scarce areas, can help motivate residents to convert lawns to biodiversity-friendly gardens.

Some goals can be achieved by coordinating with programs that are already responsible for urban greening. For example, urban forestry programs can align with biodiversity goals by setting targets for native tree planting. City stormwater programs are increasingly interested in incorporating green infrastructure into streetscapes to minimize runoff and treat contaminants. Features such as bioswales and flood detention basins can enhance local ecology by including plant palettes specific to particular habitat zones.

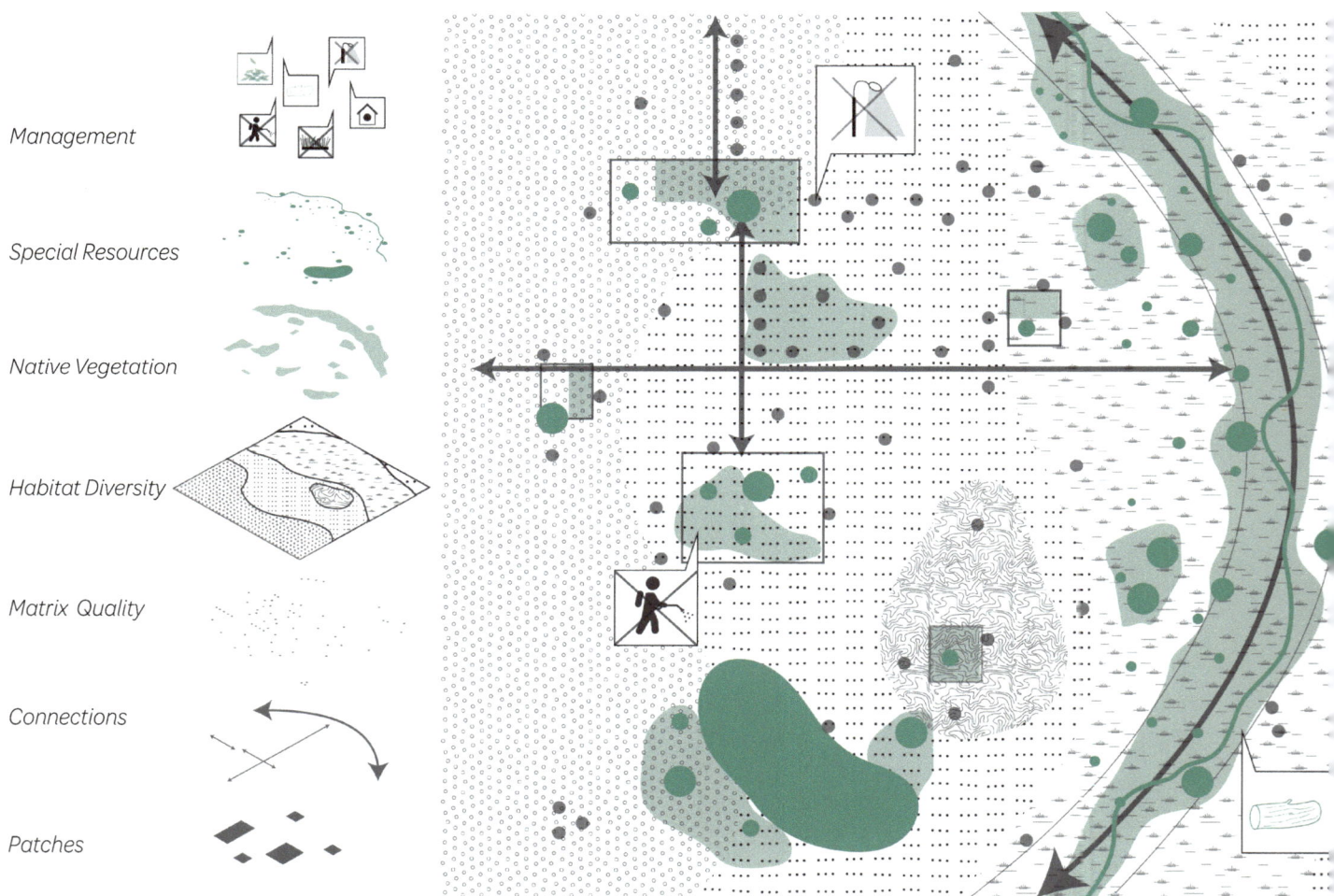

Management

Special Resources

Native Vegetation

Habitat Diversity

Matrix Quality

Connections

Patches

Urban biodiversity planning will be most effective if it includes all seven elements. Integrated across the landscape, these seven elements will work together to help build broad support for biodiversity.

Bioswales can incorporate trees, and flood detention basins can be combined with wetland restoration to re-create locally rare habitat types. In some cases, coordination among city programs can be achieved using policy frameworks. The City of San Francisco Board of Supervisors, for example, passed a resolution in 2018 that identifies biodiversity protection as a city priority (SF Environment 2018). The resolution establishes a framework for inter-agency collaboration and sharing of best practices, and promotes the conservation of biodiversity as part of strategic operations and capital planning.

Implementing biodiversity plans may be assisted by creating mechanisms that facilitate coordination and transfer of scientific knowledge. For example, many actors in the urban landscape may lack the technical expertise required to implement best practices for biodiversity. Scientific boundary organizations that bridge the gap between science and its application can play an important role in facilitating the transfer of technical information needed to apply biodiversity planning across a variety of land use types and urban greening practices (Guston 2001). In other cases, the collective impact model could also be used to create effective cross-sector coordination. In this model, a backbone organization dedicates staff to coordination among actors that work together to achieve a common agenda (Kania and Kramer 2011). This type of collaboration can be effective because it incorporates a common goal into many different types of activities through a mutually reinforcing plan of action. This model may be particularly effective in biodiversity planning given the inherent need for cross-sector and multi-stakeholder activities to achieve integrated biodiversity actions across a multitude of land use types.

We recognize that not all cities will have the resources or in-house technical capacity to conduct a full analysis of the urban biodiversity elements, or to implement all aspects of a biodiversity plan. Given that patches and corridors are two of the most important drivers of urban biodiversity, biodiversity planning initiatives could start by identifying district and site-scale opportunities to draw on these landscape features. For example, large patches and regional corridors are likely already providing support for urban biodiversity, and can be built upon, improved, and expanded. In addition, habitat zones, patches of native trees, special resources, and remnant patches of habitat can be identified in order to prioritize among land acquisition and biodiversity improvement projects.

Creating an urban biodiversity strategy

Creating an urban biodiversity strategy is an exercise that any entity could undertake, from a neighborhood organization to a city planning department. The process of creating a biodiversity strategy has many benefits, including defining goals for biodiversity, creating public support for projects, and aligning biodiversity goals with other synergistic priorities. Creating a plan can also be conducted directly with a community, incorporating feedback and identifying priorities across a broad range of stakeholders. Identifying other synergistic efforts and policies can be a first step in building an implementation plan, and can help align biodiversity with other goals, increasing the likelihood of funding and support for projects.

A useful first step in the planning process is data discovery and evaluation, where existing biodiversity assets relating to each of the seven elements are identified. This phase will provide critical information and insights into where biodiversity may already be flourishing, as well as where biodiversity support is most lacking. Analysis of the existing landscape can identify features such as regional corridors and patches, as well as park-poor areas or areas of low canopy cover. Biodiversity actions can be beneficial wherever they are implemented, and should seek broad coverage that both enriches areas low in biodiversity support and increases connections across the landscape.

With data acquired during the discovery phase, a variety of tools can be used to create a plan that increases connectivity, adds to and creates new patches, and improves the overall quality of the matrix across the planning area. For example, land acquisition can create new parks in park-poor areas and can be used to fill gaps in corridors. Existing parks can be enhanced by identifying appropriate habitat types, managing for biodiversity, and protecting special resources. Integrating across all seven elements of the framework is key to creating a successful plan, and identifying a range of options for implementing each element can help maximize the spatial coverage of a plan. The following toolkit highlights the many types of opportunities that can be incorporated into the planning process. While no plan is likely to use every item in this toolkit, most are common across many cities, and provide a starting point for the creative planning process.

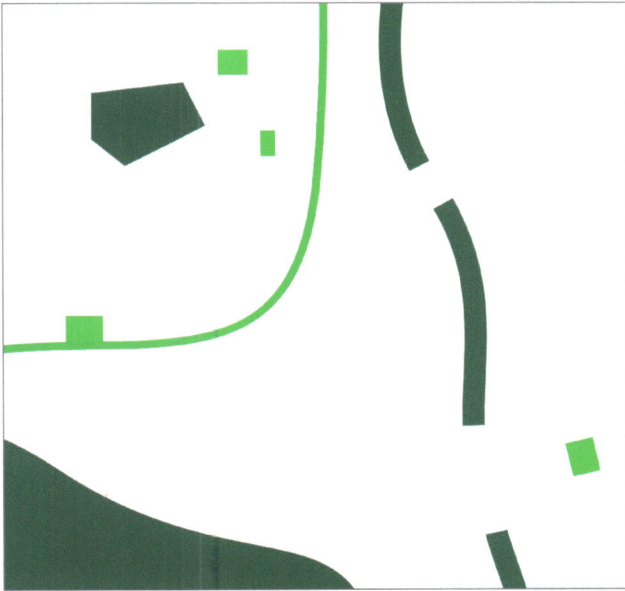

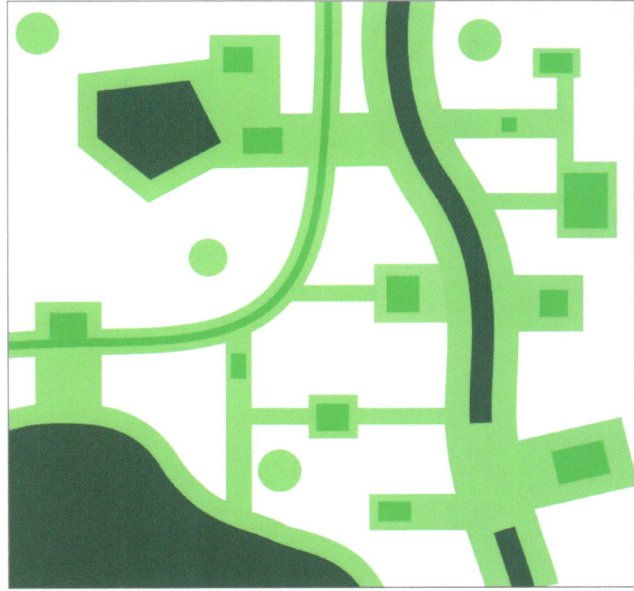

■	*Regional Hub*
■	*Local Hub*
■	*Matrix*
●	*Habitat Complex*

Developing an urban biodiversity plan can start with identifying existing resources, such as large parks and regional corridors. These features can be built upon, improved, and expanded. Areas that lack biodiversity resources can be identified and improved, and connectivity can be enhanced. These actions can be achieved through a combination of land acquisition, matrix improvements, and biodiversity-friendly management. The following pages provide a toolkit including the types of opportunities that can be identified, along with strategies for associated actions that could form the foundation of a biodiversity planning process.

Neighborhood in New Orleans, LA (Photo courtesy of Robin Grossinger)

TOOLKIT OF BIODIVERSITY ACTIONS

Existing high-quality patches

Approach: **Preserve and conserve existing open spaces**, in particular remnants of native habitat, that already provide valuable habitat. These spaces can also offer unique recreation and restorative opportunities for people that live in urban areas.

Areas with few or no greenspaces

Approach: **Acquire or dedicate land to create new patches**. Vacant lots, parking lots, post-industrial sites and other spaces can be repurposed as natural assets. Patch creation in underserved, park-poor neighborhoods can also have a positive social impact.

Greenspaces with room to grow

Approach: **Acquire land that is adjacent to existing patches** to increase their effective size. Easements and land use restrictions along patches are another mechanism for expanding patches without changes in ownership.

Infrastructure corridors

Approach: **Create new corridors** to improve connectivity between patches, or regionally, across the urban landscape. Opportunities can be found along existing infrastructure, under freeways, on easements, and along decommissioned rail tracks and other single-use linear spaces.

Narrow connections

Approach: **Expand corridors** by acquiring land along existing corridors to increase their effective width. Widening corridors can improve connectivity between patches while providing other benefits. For example, increasing setbacks from waterways can reduce flooding in urban areas and improve public access.

Fragmented connections

Approach: Strategically **acquire land to fill gaps** along existing corridors. Daylighting creeks, building wildlife crossings and extending greenways are some examples of gap-filling actions.

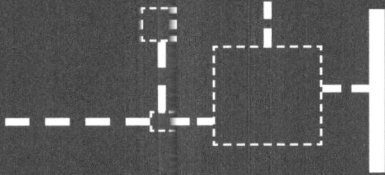

Planning for redevelopment, expansion, or development

Approach: **Incorporate biodiversity actions early in the design process**. For example, master planning for large areas of land present an opportunity to both accommodate development and augment urban biodiversity support. Creating biodiversity networks is most effective during early phases of design, when there is most flexibility in the location of buildings and infrastructure.

Existing open spaces with large opportunities for improvement

Approach: **Upgrade existing open spaces** to better support native flora and fauna, particularly through the inclusion of diverse habitat types, special resources, and native plantings. Spaces that are currently dominated by extensive lawns, impervious areas, or exotic plantings all present opportunities to improve biodiversity support.

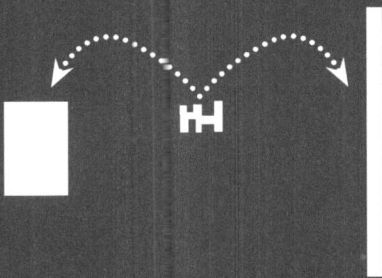

Privately-managed residential spaces

Approach: Facilitate and promote programs that support **residential actions that benefit biodiversity.** Lawn conversion incentive programs, wildlife-friendly and drought-friendly gardening certification programs, and university cooperative extension programs all provide incentives and opportunities for outreach. Coordinated efforts on private land can create habitat complexes that function as stepping stones and enhance connectivity in the urban landscape.

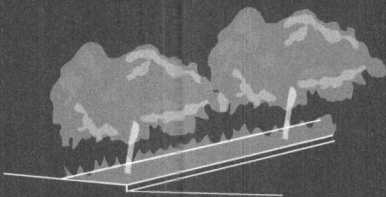

Treeless streets

Approach: Use opportunities for **streetscape re-design** to reduce barriers and improve connectivity between larger features. Adding native street trees, widening planting areas, integrating stormwater features, and reducing travel lanes can help support the movement of species and deliver a wide range of ecosystem benefits for people.

Synergies with other urban greening efforts

Urban biodiversity presents a largely untapped opportunity to generate greater public support for urban open space and greening investments. While urban ecology and biodiversity are frequently listed as an intended benefit of urban greening, the justification and expected results are often not well-developed or compelling. Showing how urban forestry, stormwater, landscape design, and other efforts contribute to the ecological health of the city, including specific much-appreciated local flora and fauna, can connect these initiatives to broader values and generate a new constituency of support.

A variety of urban greening initiatives are already underway in many cities. Some cities are creating green infrastructure plans to guide the installation of bioswales and rain gardens to reduce contaminants in urban runoff. Other cities are creating climate action plans to mitigate greenhouse gas emissions and adapt to a changing climate. City general plans, green infrastructure requirements, urban forest master plans, parks master plans, and other guidance documents regularly update policy for many of the key features in a biodiverse city. These planning and policy efforts could benefit from incorporating biodiversity planning as a key goal or, when biodiversity is mentioned providing more specific recommendations and expectations. Given the many competing priorities for physical space and financial resources in urban landscapes, biodiversity planning will benefit from a stronger technical foundation to identify and support specific high-value actions.

At the same time, the array of different kinds of urban greening initiatives offers immense opportunity to implement significant biodiversity improvements. State-mandated plans for climate change adaptation and water quality improvement present an opportunity to incorporate biodiversity objectives and create efficient, multi-benefit plans for resilient cities. For example, tidal marsh restoration can buffer shores against rising seas while providing critical habitat for a range of marsh plants and animals. Bicycle and pedestrian-friendly street improvements designed with nature can enhance ecological connectivity while delivering shade and nature access that increase the usage and health benefits of the greenway. With the right plant palette and specifications, green infrastructure can both manage stormwater runoff and support local wildlife. Existing and new policy frameworks, best practices, outreach activities, and ongoing infrastructure upgrades can all be harnessed to achieve biodiversity goals. In addition, incentives and regulatory structures can be directed towards biodiversity. For example, stormwater permitting processes and regulatory structures related to water quality improvement can be written to include targets for urban greening that encourage green infrastructure projects.

In semi-arid climates where water scarcity is a key concern, native plants can help meet new expectations for water consumption in public and private landscapes. For example, in California, native oaks epitomize the multiple benefits of native plant selection. They support local biodiversity, store more carbon than most urban trees, provide large canopies, and require little water (Spotswood et al. 2017). Urban biodiversity can also contribute to urban food production, as native flowering plants can support pollinating insects that are crucial to the success of urban agriculture (Davis et al. 2017). Urban greening—including the integration of biodiversity patches,

Traffic Circle with native vegetation in Berkeley, CA (Photo courtesy of Shira Bezalel)

corridors, and matrix improvements—can be linked to a remarkably diverse range of important cultural and biophysical ecosystem services, including spiritual enrichment, cognitive development, reflection, recreation, aesthetic experience, as well as stormwater management, heat island mitigation, pollution control, and carbon sequestration (Plieninger et al. 2015, Livesley et al. 2016).

As cities are redesigned to support more people and adapt to climate change, it will be increasingly essential to design the disparate urban green features and spaces to work together to achieve these multiple functions. By aligning urban forestry, stormwater and flood protection, greenways, parks, and public/private landscaping, communities can create networks of nature that maximize the delivery of critical ecological functions to all parts of the city. The science of urban biodiversity provides a technical framework to integrate nature into urban design and to leverage disparate small and large initiatives to generate greater health, ecology, and resilience.

Overcoming Challenges to Designing for Biodiversity

Development of urban greenspaces with an eye towards biodiversity can have multiple benefits for both nature and people (Dearborn and Kark 2010). Mental and physical health benefits for people with exposure to greenspaces are well documented (Hartig et al. 2014, van den Berg et al. 2015) and there is evidence that increased biodiversity can enhance the health benefits derived from these spaces (Fuller et al. 2007). Additionally, urban greenspaces are where many urban residents will have their primary day-to-day interactions with nature, which can be foundational in creating connections to the local environment and motivating environmental stewardship (Cleary et al. 2018, Whitburn et al. 2018). Particular attention to native species can further increase the value of these interactions by facilitating local connections and helping to create unique regional character. As with biodiversity, special features such as large trees in urban areas can have outsized impacts on people (Cox et al. 2019).

While there are numerous benefits to be derived from urban nature, biodiversity also comes with trade-offs that should be considered part of project implementation. Emphasizing the varied benefits for people when designing and promoting features for biodiversity may improve public opinion of these efforts and increase the likelihood of their success.

One important consideration when improving habitat and connectivity for wildlife in urban areas is the potential for human-wildlife conflict. Increasing opportunities for interactions between animals and people can have both positive and negative outcomes (Soulsbury and White 2015, Cox and Gaston 2018). While biodiversity hubs and large greenspaces are ideal places to support carnivorous mammals, for example, their dispersal into more heavily populated areas may lead to conflict, with negative outcomes for both people and wildlife. Feeding of wildlife can exacerbate problems of conflict with wildlife by habituating animals to human contact. Resident attitudes towards particular animals, such as those perceived as dangerous or destructive, may result in pushback against efforts to support urban wildlife. Careful planning for sensitive species in combination with education and outreach can help address and mitigate these concerns.

Evaluating which biodiversity elements can be applied in which parts of the city can also help achieve broad biodiversity benefits while also accommodating community needs for particular spaces. All steps of the proposed biodiversity framework do not have to be carried out in all parts of a city to support considerable biodiversity, and targeting the types of interventions to spaces where they are most appropriate can go a long way towards mitigating potential conflicts. For example, while urban residents may not welcome carnivorous mammals in their backyards, they may be happy to see these animals in larger greenspaces. Dead trees may be unacceptable near businesses or houses, but may be less of a problem in larger greenspaces in areas with little foot traffic. Small areas such as road medians, traffic circles, and vacant lots may be good targets for removing lawns and planting for biodiversity as long as aesthetics are maintained, while recreation fields and social spaces may be less practical to convert.

Adoption of biodiversity interventions in private spaces depends strongly on the attitudes and behavior of individual landowners, and while education is important, it is often not sufficient to promote environmental actions and values (Byerly et al. 2018). There has been some success using interactive dialog intervention to improve resident knowledge of and attitudes towards biodiversity (van Heezik et al. 2012). van Heezik and co-authors conducted these dialogues with private homeowners. Going beyond general education, interventions included specific information about each participant's individual garden, and each homeowner was told how their garden ranked in terms of biodiversity benefits compared to others. Participants who received this feedback did not change deeply-held environmental values. However, many demonstrated an improved understanding of their yard as habitat for wildlife and reported making changes to their gardening practices. If such intensive, targeted actions cannot be conducted everywhere, they can be directed towards high-priority areas for conservation, such as near biodiversity hubs or in potential habitat complexes.

Social norms, as well as the behaviors and expectations of others, can have important impacts on whether individuals choose to act in environmentally beneficial ways (Byerly et al. 2018). People may be more likely to take action to support biodiversity if they perceive that others in their community agree and that these actions would be considered socially acceptable or valuable (Nassauer et al. 2009, Hunter et al. 2012, Goddard et al. 2013). Biodiversity outreach can use this information proactively. Including information related to existing community support for biodiversity actions may help achieve greater support and participation.

Individual opinions can also be influenced by the particular history of a place, and these opinions can change over time. Understanding the social and historical context of a place can help identify barriers and opportunities. Working directly with communities to plan biodiversity projects will often reveal this important context and can help in designing successful interventions. External events such as droughts, development, and natural disasters can lead to rapid shifts in public opinion, sometimes providing new opportunities to make changes for biodiversity. Incentive programs associated with these events can help promote change. However, formal incentive programs are often less effective than informal social pressures, and should be employed strategically where money has been identified as an important barrier (Goddard et al. 2013).

In other cases, exploring how biodiversity goals can be aligned with an individual's priorities for their yard can lead to targeted solutions that overcome particular barriers or concerns. For example, a program might emphasize the reduced maintenance needs of native plants for managers motivated by a desire for low maintenance landscaping. Where recreation is a priority, native plant gardens can be designed in combination with areas of functional lawn. For residents concerned about aesthetics and community opinion, informative signs about native plant gardens can help communicate to neighbors that an untidy-looking space is purposeful and cared for.

Understanding the social dynamics and drivers of individual decisions in private spaces is an important component of creating a successful plan for biodiversity conservation in urban contexts. Anticipating potential challenges and including plans to address them can lead to more effective urban biodiversity projects. Given the many benefits of access to diverse greenspaces, it is worthwhile to design these interventions in ways that will be feasible and successful in a wide variety of communities and contexts. §

5

LOOKING FORWARD

Cities will face significant challenges over the coming decades as they work to accommodate population growth and adapt to a changing climate. After a century or more of development, cities around the world have inherited legacies that put little priority on leaving space for nature. There is growing recognition that integrating nature back into cities is critical for creating livable places that can weather the coming changes. However, there is still a long way to go towards making a new vision for cities a reality.

To get there will require cross-sector collaborative approaches, bottom-up community based projects, and broad dissemination of the scientific results that support the case for nature in cities. The Urban Biodiversity Framework provides a scientifically-based foundation for these efforts that can help guide the different actors and sectors that shape urban morphology to be more supportive of local ecosystems and species. We envision these principles informing a variety of actions and scales, from regional mobility or climate adaptation plans to backyard planting palettes, through a combination of both targeted and holistic strategies.

Urban biodiversity, and the diverse benefits it can provide, offers a framework for linking urban spaces into a functional network that everyone can contribute to. Our vision is that urban biodiversity planning can unite people, creating a shared agenda where each actor can have a role in shaping healthier cities where everyone stands to gain. §

REFERENCES

[ABAG] Association of Bay Area Governments. 2006. Land Use dataset. Accessed from abag.ca.gov, 2018-5-1.

Agosta SJ. 2006. On ecological fitting, plant-insect associations, herbivore host shifts, and host plant selection. *Oikos* 114(3):556–565.

Ahern J. 2013. Urban landscape sustainability and resilience: the promise and challenges of integrating ecology with urban planning and design. Landscape Ecology 28(6):1203–1212.

[AIS] Aerial Information Systems. 2010. Santa Clara Valley Water District Vegetation Mapping Report for Stream Management Program. Prepared for Santa Clara Valley Water District, July 2010.

Aitken SN, Whitlock MC. 2013. Assisted gene flow to facilitate local adaptation to climate change. *Annual Review of Ecology, Evolution, and Systematics* 44(1):367–388.

Angold PG, Sadler JP, Hill MO, Pullin A, Rushton S, Austin K, Small E, Wood B, Wadsworth R, Sanderson R, et al. 2006. Biodiversity in urban habitat patches. *Science of The Total Environment* 360(1–3):196–204.

Arca E, Battisti C, Fraticelli F. 2012. Area-effect in breeding bird communities occurring in an archipelago of urban holm oak fragments (Rome, Central Italy). *Vie Milieu* :6.

Aronson MFJ, La Sorte FA, Nilon CH, Katti M, Goddard MA, Lepczyk CA, Warren PS, Williams NSG, Cilliers S, Clarkson B, et al. 2014. A global analysis of the impacts of urbanization on bird and plant diversity reveals key anthropogenic drivers. Proceedings of the Royal Society B: Biological Sciences 281(1780):20133330–20133330.

Aronson MFJ, Nilon CH, Lepczyk CA, Parker TS, Warren PS, Cilliers SS, Goddard MA, Hahs AK, Herzog C, Katti M, et al. 2016. Hierarchical filters determine community assembly of urban species pools. Ecology 97(11):2952–2963.

Aronson MF, Lepczyk CA, Evans KL, Goddard MA, Lerman SB, MacIvor JS, Nilon CH, Vargo T. 2017. Biodiversity in the city: key challenges for urban greenspace management. *Frontiers in Ecology and the Environment* 15(4):189–196.

[BAARI] San Francisco Estuary Institute. 2017. Bay Area Aquatic Resource Inventory. Version 2.1. San Francisco Estuary Institute, Richmond, CA. Accessed May 2018.

Baldwin BG. 2014. Origins of plant diversity in the California Floristic Province. *Annual Review of Ecology, Evolution, and Systematics* 45(1):347–369.

Baldwin BG, Thornhill AH, Freyman WA, Ackerly DD, Kling MM, Morueta-Holme N, Mishler BD. 2017. Species richness and endemism in the native flora of California. *American Journal of Botany* 104(3):487–501.

Barbour M, Keeler-Wolf T, Schoenherr AA. 2007. Terrestrial vegetation of California. Third edition. Univ of California Press, 2007.

Bartholomew F. 2000. Aneides lugubris: arboreal salamander. Accessed from https://animaldiversity.org/accounts/Aneides_lugubris/.

Bartomeus I, Frund J, Williams N. 2016. Invasive plants as novel food resources, the pollinators' perspective. Biological Invasions and Animal Behavior. Cambridge.

Bateman PW, Fleming PA. 2012. Big city life: carnivores in urban environments: Urban carnivores. *Journal of Zoology* 287(1):1–23.

Batten KM, Scow KM, Davies KF, Harrison SP. 2006. Two invasive plants alter soil microbial community composition in serpentine grasslands. *Biological Invasions* 8(2):217–230.

Baum KA, Haynes KJ, Dillemuth FP, Cronin JT. 2004. The matrix enhances the effectiveness of corridors and stepping stones. *Ecology* 85(10):2671–2676.

Beier P. 1995. Dispersal of juvenile cougars in fragmented habitat. *The Journal of Wildlife Management* 59(2):228.

Belaire JA, Whelan CJ, Minor ES. 2014. Having our yards and sharing them too: the collective effects of yards on native bird species in an urban landscape. *Ecological Applications* 24(8):2132–2143.

Beller E, Salomon M, Grossinger R. 2010. Historical vegetation and drainage patterns of western Santa Clara Valley: A technical memorandum describing landscape ecology in Lower Peninsula, West Valley, and Guadalupe Watershed Management Areas.

Beninde J, Feldmeier S, Werner M, Peroverde D, Schulte U, Hochkirch A, Veith M. 2016. Cityscape genetics: structural vs. functional connectivity of an urban lizard population. *Molecular Ecology* 25(20):4984–5000.

Beninde J, Veith M, Hochkirch A. 2015. Biodiversity in cities needs space: a meta-analysis of factors determining intra-urban biodiversity variation. *Ecology Letters* 18(6):581–592.

Bertin RI. 2002. Losses of Native Plant Species from Worcester, Massachusetts. 104:26.

Birdlife International 2018. 2018. The IUCN Red List of Threatened Species 2018: e.T22679603A131906420. Accessed from http://dx.doi.org/10.2305/IUCN.UK.2018-2.RLTS.T22679603A131906420.en., 2019-2-28.

Björklund M, Ruiz I, Senar JC. 2010. Genetic differentiation in the urban habitat: the great tits (Parus major) of the parks of Barcelona city. *Biological Journal of the Linnean Society* 99(1):9–19.

Bjorkman J, Thorne JH, Hollander A, Roth NE, Boynton RM, de Goede J, Xiao Q, Beardsley K, McPherson G, Quinn JE. 2015. Biomass, carbon sequestration, and avoided emissions: assessing the role of urban trees in California. Report of the UC Davis Statewide Assessment of Urban Forests Project to the California Fire Urban and Community Forestry Program. Information Center for the Environment, University of California, Davis.

Blair RB. 1996. Land use and avian species diversity along an urban gradient. *Ecological Applications* 6(2):506–519.

Bolger D. 2002. Habitat fragmentation effects on birds in Southern California: contrast to the top-down paradigm. Studies in Avian Biology 25:141–157.

Bousman W. 2007. Breeding bird atlas of Santa Clara County, California.

Bradley CA, Altizer S. 2007. Urbanization and the ecology of wildlife diseases. *Trends in Ecology & Evolution* 22(2):95–102.

Brandt L, Derby Lewis A, Fahey R, Scott L, Darling L, Swanston C. 2016. A framework for adapting urban forests to climate change. Environmental Science & Policy 66:393–402.

Brooker RW, Maestre FT, Callaway RM, Lortie CL, Cavieres LA, Kunstler G, Liancourt P, Tielbörger K, Travis JMJ, Anthelme F, et al. 2007. Facilitation in plant communities: the past, the present, and the future. Journal of Ecology 0(0):070908024102002-???

Brown LM, Graham CH. 2015. Demography, traits and vulnerability to urbanization: can we make generalizations? *Journal of Applied Ecology* 52(6):1455–1464.

Browning M, Rigolon A. 2018. Do Income, Race and ethnicity, and sprawl influence the greenspace-human health link in city-level analyses? Findings from 496 cities in the United States. *International Journal of Environmental Research and Public Health* 15(7):1541.

Byerly H, Balmford A, Ferraro PJ, Hammond Wagner C, Palchak E, Polasky S, Ricketts TH, Schwartz AJ, Fisher B. 2018. Nudging pro-environmental behavior: evidence and opportunities. Frontiers in Ecology and the Environment 16(3):159–168.

Cadenasso ML, Pickett STA, Schwarz K. 2007. Spatial heterogeneity in urban ecosystems: reconceptualizing land cover and a framework for classification. *Frontiers in Ecology and the Environment* 5(2):80–88.

Callaghan C, Lyons M, Martin J, Major R, Kingsford R. 2017. Assessing the reliability of avian biodiversity measures of urban greenspaces using eBird citizen science data. *Avian Conservation & Ecology* 12(2).

(Canopy) Canopy trees for Palo Alto. 2002. The Oakwell Survey: A definitive survey of the native oaks of Palo Alto. Canopy trees for Palo Alto. Accessed from http://canopy.org/wp-content/uploads/OakWell_Survey.pdf, 2018-5-1.

Cardoso GC. 2014. Nesting and acoustic ecology, but not phylogeny, influence passerine urban tolerance. *Global Change Biology* 20(3):803–810.

Carreiro MM, Howe K, Parkhurst DF, Pouyat RV. 1999. Variation in quality and decomposability of red oak leaf litter along an urban-rural gradient. *Biology and Fertility of Soils* 30(3):258–268.

Cates D, Allen N. 2002. Build Nest Boxes for Wild Birds.

[CCED] California Conservation Easement Database. 2016. Accessed from www.calands.org, 2018-5-1.

Chapin III FS, Zava eta ES, Eviner VT, Naylor RL, Vitousek PM, Reynolds HL, Hooper DU, Lavorel S, Sala O E, Hobbie SE, et al. 2000. Consequences of changing biodiversity. *Nature* 405(6783):234–242.

Charter M, Meyrom K, Leshem Y, Aviel S, Izhaki I, Motro Y. 2010. Does nest box location and orientation affect occupation rate and breeding success of barn owls *Tyto alba* in a semi-arid environment? *Acta Ornithologica* 45(1):115–119.

Cleary A, Fielding KS, Murray Z, Roiko A. 2018. Predictors of nature connection among urban residents: assessing the role of childhood and adult nature experiences. Environment and Behavior :001391651881143.

Clergeau P, Savard J-PL, Mennechez G, Falardeau G. 1998. Bird abundance and diversity along an urban-rural gradient: a comparative study between two cities on different continents. *The Condor* 100(3):413–425.

Connor EF, McCoy ED. 1979. The statistics and biology of the species-area relationship. *The American Naturalist* 113(6):791–833.

Cornell HV. 1985. Local and regional richness of Cynipine gall wasps on California oaks. *Ecology* 66(4):1247–1260.

Cornell Lab of Ornithology. 2019. Birds of North America. Accessed from https://birdsna.org/Species-Account/bna/home, 2019-2-28.

Costello LR, Hagen BW, Jones KS. 2011. *Oaks in the urban landscape: selection, care, and preservation*. Richmond, CA: University of California Agriculture and Natural Resources.

County of Santa Clara, City of San Jose, City of Gilroy, Santa Clara Valley Water District, Santa Clara Valley Transportation Authority. 2012. Final Santa Clara Valley habitat plan. Santa Clara County, California.

Cox DTC, Bennie J, Casalegno S, Hudson HL, Anderson K, Gaston KJ. 2019. Skewed contributions of individual trees to indirect nature experiences. Landscape and Urban Planning 185:28–34.

Cox DTC, Gaston KJ. 2016. Urban bird feeding: connecting people with nature. *PLOS ONE* 11(7):e0158717

Cox DTC, Gaston KJ. 2018. Human–nature interactions and the consequences and drivers of provisioning wildlife. Philosophical Transactions of the Royal Society B: Biological Sciences 373(1745):20170092.

[CPAD] California Protected Areas Database 2017a. Accessed from www.calands.org, 2018-5-1.

Craves JA. 2009. A fifteen-year study of fall stopover patterns of Catharus thrushes at an inland, urban site. *The Wilson Journal of Ornithology* 121(1):112–118.

Currin CA, Davis J, Malhotra A. 2017. Response of salt marshes to wave energy provides guidance for successful living shoreline implementation. In Bilkovic DM, Mitchell MM, La Peyre MK, Toft JD (eds), Living Shorelines, 211–234. Boca Raton, FL : Taylor & Francis, 2017. | Series: Marine: CRC Press.

Dahlgren RA, Horwath WR, Tate KW, Camping TJ. 2003. Blue oak enhance soil quality in California oak woodlands. *California Agriculture* 57(2):42–47.

Dahlgren RA, Singer MJ, Huang X. 1997. Oak tree and grazing impacts on soil properties and nutrients in a California oak woodland. 39(1):20.

D'Antonio C, Malmstorm C, Reynolds S, Gerlach J. 2007. Ecology of invasive non-native species in California grassland. California Grasslands: Ecology and Management. University of California Press, Berkeley, California, USA.

Davis A, Taylor CE, Major RE. 2012. Seasonal abundance and habitat use of Australian parrots in an urbanised landscape. *Landscape and Urban Planning* 106(2):191–198.

Davis AY, Lonsdorf EV, Shierk CR, Matteson KC, Taylor JR, Lovell ST, Minor ES. 2017. Enhancing pollination supply in an urban ecosystem through landscape modifications. *Landscape and Urban Planning* 162:157–166.

Dearborn DC, Kark S. 2010. Motivations for conserving urban biodiversity. Conservation Biology 24(2):432–440.

Dennis M, James P. 2016. User participation in urban green commons: exploring the links between access, voluntarism, biodiversity and well being. Urban Forestry & Urban Greening 15:22–31.

Devictor V, Julliard R, Jiguet F. 2008. Distribution of specialist and generalist species along spatial gradients of habitat disturbance and fragmentation. *Oikos* 0(0):080211051304426–0.

Donofrio J, Kuhn Y, McWalter K, Winsor M. 2009. Water-sensitive urban design: an emerging model in sustainable design and comprehensive water-cycle management. *Environmental Practice* 11(3):179–189.

Drinnan IN. 2005. The search for fragmentation thresholds in a southern Sydney suburb. *Biological Conservation* 124(3):339–349.

Driscoll DA, Banks SC, Barton PS, Lindenmayer DB, Smith AL. 2013. Conceptual domain of the matrix in fragmented landscapes. *Trends in Ecology & Evolution* 28(10):605–613.

Duarte CM, Losada IJ, Hendriks IE, Mazarrasa I, Marbà N. 2013. The role of coastal plant communities for climate change mitigation and adaptation. *Nature Climate Change* 3(11):961–968.

Dures SG, Cumming GS. 2010. The confounding influence of homogenising invasive species in a globally endangered and largely urban biome: Does habitat quality dominate avian biodiversity? *Biological Conservation* 143(3):768–777.

eBird. 2019. eBird: An online database of bird distribution and abundance [web application]. eBird, Ithaca, New York. Available: http://www.ebird.org.

Ehrlich PR, Raven PH. 1964. Butterflies and plants: a study in coevolution. *Evolution* 18(4):586–608.

Er KBH, Innes JL, Martin K, Klinkenberg B. 2005. Forest loss with urbanization predicts bird extirpations in Vancouver. *Biological Conservation* 126(3):410–419.

Erickson WP, Johnson GD, Jr DPY. 2005. A summary and comparison of bird mortality from anthropogenic causes with an emphasis on collisions. :15.

Escobedo FJ, Kroeger T, Wagner JE. 2011. Urban forests and pollution mitigation: analyzing ecosystem services and disservices. *Environmental pollution* 159(8):2078–2087.

Evans KL, Chamberlain DE, Hatchwell BJ, Gregory RD, Gaston KJ. 2011. What makes an urban bird? *Global Change Biology* 17(1):32–44.

Evans MJ, Banks SC, Driscoll DA, Hicks AJ, Melbourne BA, Davies KF. 2017. Short- and long-term effects of habitat fragmentation differ but are predicted by response to the matrix. *Ecology* 98(2):807–819.

Faeth SH, Bang C, Saari S. 2011. Urban biodiversity: patterns and mechanisms. *Annals of the New York Academy of Sciences* 1223(1):69–81.

Faeth SH, Warren PS, Shochat E, Marussich WA. 2005. Trophic dynamics in urban communities. *BioScience* 55(5):399–407.

Fang C-F, Ling D-L. 2003. Investigation of the noise reduction provided by tree belts. *Landscape and Urban Planning* 63(4):187–195.

Favaro C, Moore JW. 2015. Fish assemblages and barriers in an urban stream network. *Freshwater Science* 34(3):991–1005.

Feeley KJ, Rehm EM, Machovina B. 2012. The responses of tropical forest species to global climate change: acclimate, adapt, migrate, or go extinct? *Frontiers of Biogeography* 4(2).

Felson AJ, Pickett ST. 2005. Designed experiments: new approaches to studying urban ecosystems. Frontiers in Ecology and the Environment 3(10):549–556.

Fernandez-Juricic E. 2000. Avifaunal use of wooded streets in an urban landscape. *Conservation Biology* 14(2):513–521.

Fite K, Smiley ET, McIntyre J, Wells CE. 2011. Evaluation of a soil decompaction and amendment process for urban trees. :8.

Forman RTT. 2016. Urban ecology principles: are urban ecology and natural area ecology really different? *Landscape Ecology* 31(8):1653–1662.

Fuller RA, Irvine KN, Devine-Wright P, Warren PH, Gaston KJ. 2007. Psychological benefits of greenspace increase with biodiversity. *Biology Letters* 3(4):390–394.

Gallagher RV, Makinson RO, Hogbin PM, Hancock N. 2015. Assisted colonization as a climate change adaptation tool. Austral Ecology 40(1):12–20.

Galloway D, Jones D, Ingebritsen S. 1999. Land subsidence in the United States. *US Geological Survey Survey* 1182.

Garden JG, Mcalpine CA, Possingham HP, Jones DN. 2007. Habitat structure is more important than vegetation composition for local-level management of native terrestrial reptile and small mammal species living in urban remnants: a case study from Brisbane, Australia. *Austral Ecology* 32(6):669–685.

Gaston KJ, Smith RM, Thompson K, Warren PH. 2005. Urban domestic gardens (II): experimental tests of methods for increasing biodiversity. *Biodiversity and Conservation* 14(2):395–413.

Geiger M, Taucher AL, Gloor S, Hegglin D, Bontadina F. 2018. In the footsteps of city foxes: evidence for a rise of urban badger populations in Switzerland. *Hystrix It. J. Mamm* 29(2).

Gilbert-Norton L, Wilson R, Stevens JR, Beard KH. 2010. A meta-analytic review of corridor effectiveness: corridor meta-analysis. *Conservation Biology* 24(3):660–668.

Gledhill DG, James P, Davies DH. 2008. Pond density as a determinant of aquatic species richness in an urban landscape. *Landscape Ecology* 23(10):1219–1230.

Goddard MA, Dougill AJ, Benton TG. 2010. Scaling up from gardens: biodiversity conservation in urban environments. *Trends in Ecology & Evolution* 25(2):90–98.

Goddard MA, Dougill AJ, Benton TG. 2013. Why garden for wildlife? Social and ecological drivers, motivations and barriers for biodiversity management in residential landscapes. Ecological Economics 86:258–273.

Goddard MA, Ikin K, Lerman SB. 2017. Ecological and social factors determining the diversity of birds in residential yards and gardens. In Murgui E, Hedblom M (eds), Ecology and conservation of birds in urban environments, 371–397. Cham: Springer International Publishing.

Gómez-Baggethun E, Gren Å, Barton DN, Langemeyer J, McPhearson T, O'Farrell P, Andersson E, Hamstead Z, Kremer P. 2013. Urban ecosystem services. In Elmqvist T, Fragkias M, Goodness J, et al. (eds), Urbanization, biodiversity and ecosystem services: challenges and opportunities: a global assessment, 175–251. Dordrecht: Springer Netherlands.

Greco SE, Airola DA. 2018. The importance of native valley oaks (Quercus lobata) as stopover habitat for migratory songbirds in urban Sacramento, California, USA. Urban Forestry & Urban Greening 29:303–311.

Greene CS, Robinson PJ, Millward AA. 2018. Canopy of advantage: who benefits most from city trees? *Journal of Environmental Management* 208:24–35.

Griffin JR, Critchfield WB. 1972. The distribution of forest trees in California. Res. Paper PSW-RP-82. Berkeley, CA: Pacific Southwest Forest and Range Experiment Station, Forest Service, US Department of Agriculture; 60 p, 82.

Grimm NB, Faeth SH, Golubiewski NE, Redman CL, Wu J, Bai X, Briggs JM. 2008. Global change and the ecology of cities. *Science* 319(5864):756–760.

Grossinger R, Askevold R, Striplen C, Brewster E, Pearce S, Cayce K, McKee L, Collins J. 2006. Coyote Creek watershed historical ecology study: historical conditions and landscape change in the eastern Santa Clara County, California.

Grossinger R, Beller E, Salomon M, Whipple A, Askevold R, Striplen C, Brewster E, Leidy R. 2008. South Santa Clara Valley historical study, including Soap Lake, the Upper Pajaro River, and Llagas Uvas-Carnadero, and Pacheco Creeks.

Guston DH. 2001. Boundary organizations in environmental policy and science: an introduction. *Science, Technology, & Human Values* 26(4):399–408.

Hagan J, Grove S. 1999. Coarse woody debris. *Journal of Forestry* 97(1).

Hails CJ, Kavanagh M. 2013. Bring back the birds! Planning for trees and other plants to support Southeast Asian wildlife in urban areas. The Raffles Bulletin of Zoology Supplement No. 29: 243-258.

Hamerstrom F, Hamerstrom FN, Hart J. 1973. Nest boxes: an effective management tool for kestrels. *The Journal of Wildlife Management* 37(3):400–403.

Harris EM, Polsky C, Larson KL, Garvoille R, Martin DG, Brumand J, Ogden L. 2012. Heterogeneity in residential yard care: evidence from Boston, Miami, and Phoenix. Human Ecology 40(5):735–749.

Hartig T, Mitchell R, de Vries S, Frumkin H. 2014. Nature and health. *Annual Review of Public Health* 35(1):207–228.

Hatfield R, Jepsen S, Throp R, Richardson L, Colla S. 2014. Bombus melanopygus. The IUCN Red List of Threatened Species 2014: e.T44937809A68983638. Accessed from http://dx.doi.org/10.2305/IUCN.UK.2014-3.RLTS.T44937809A68983638.en, 2019-2-28.

Hedblom M, Söderström B. 2012. Effects of urban matrix on reproductive performance of great tit (Parus major) in urban woodlands. *Urban Ecosystems* 15(1):167–180.

Heleno RH, Ceia RS, Ramos JA, Memmott J. 2009. Effects of alien plants on insect abundance and biomass a food-web approach. *Conservation Biology* 23(2):410–419.

Heller NE, Zavaleta ES. 2009. Biodiversity management in the face of climate change: a review of 22 years of recommendations. *Biological Conservation* 142(1):14–32.

Herrmann DL, Pearse IS, Baty JH. 2012. Drivers of specialist herbivore diversity across 10 cities. *Landscape and Urban Planning* 108(2):123–130.

Hill MJ, Biggs J, Thornhill I, Briers RA, Gledhill DG, White JC, Wood PJ, Hassall C. 2017. Urban ponds as an aquatic biodiversity resource in modified landscapes. *Global Change Biology* 23(3):986–999.

Hitchmough J. 2011. Exotic plants and plantings in the sustainable, designed urban landscape. *Landscape and Urban Planning* 100(4):380–382.

Hobday AJ, Minstrell ML. 2008. Distribution and abundance of roadkill on Tasmanian highways: human management options. *Wildlife Research* 35(7):712.

Hodgson P, French K, Major RE. 2007. Avian movement across abrupt ecological edges: differential responses to housing density in an urban matrix. Landscape and Urban Planning 79(3–4):266–272.

Hothem RL, Brussee BE, Davis Jr. WE. 2010. Black-crowned night heron (Nyct corax nycticorax). *The Birds of North America Online*.

Howard J, Klausmeyer K, Fesenmyer K. 2013. Below the surface: California's freshwater biodiversity. The Nature Conservancy of California, San Francisco, CA.

Hunt A, Watkiss P. 2011. Climate change impacts and adaptation in cities: a review of the literature. *Climatic Change* 104(1):13–49.

Hunter MCR, Brown DG. 2012. Spatial contagion: gardening along the street in residential neighborhoods. Landscape and Urban Planning 105(4):407–416.

Hunter ML. 2007. Climate change and moving species: furthering the debate on assisted colonization. *Conservation Biology* 21(5):1356–1358.

Ikin K, Beaty RM, Lindenmayer DB, Knight E, Fischer J, Manning AD. 2013. Pocket parks in a compact city: how do birds respond to increasing residential density? *Landscape Ecology* 28(1):45–56.

iNaturalist. 2019. Accessed from http://www.inaturalist.org, 2019-2-28.

Jackson JA, Tate J. 1974. An analysis of nest box use by purple martins, house sparrows, and starlings in eastern North America. *The Wilson Bulletin* 86(4):435–449.

Jepsen S, Schweitzer DF, Young B, Sears N, Ormes M, Black SH. 2015. Conservation status and ecology of the monarch butterfly in the United States. :36.

Jokimaki J. 1999. Occurrence of breeding bird species in urban parks: Effects of park structure and broad-scale variables. :15.

Kania J, Kramer M. 2011. Collective impact. Stanford Social Innovation Review.

Karlinsky S, Szambelan S, Wang K. 2017. Room for more: SPUR's housing agenda for San Jose. San Francisco Bay Area Planning and Urban Research Association (SPUR).

Keeley BW, Tuttle MD. 1999. Bats in American bridges: resource publication No. 4. *Bat Conservation International, Inc.*

Kendal D, Williams NSG, Williams KJH. 2012. A cultivated environment: exploring the global distribution of plants in gardens, parks and streetscapes. Urban Ecosystems 15(3):637–652.

Koenig WD, Haydock J. 1999. Oaks, acorns, and the geographical ecology of acorn woodpeckers. *Journal of Biogeography* 26(1):159–165.

Kueppers LM, Snyder MA, Sloan LC, Zavaleta ES, Fulfrost B. 2005. Modeled regional climate change and California endemic oak ranges. *Proceedings of the National Academy of Sciences* 102(45):16281–16286.

Larson KL, Casagrande D, Harlan SL, Yabiku ST. 2009. Residents' yard choices and rationales in a desert city: social priorities, ecological impacts, and decision tradeoffs. Environmental Management 44(5):921–937.

Le Roux DS, Ikin K, Lindenmayer DB, Blanchard W, Manning AD, Gibbons P. 2014. Reduced availability of habitat structures in urban landscapes: Implications for policy and practice. *Landscape and Urban Planning* 125:57–64.

Leong M, Dunn RR, Trautwein MD. 2018. Biodiversity and socioeconomics in the city: a review of the luxury effect. *Biology Letters* 14(5):20180082.

Lerman SB, Contosta AR, Milam J, Bang C. 2018. To mow or to mow less: lawn mowing frequency affects bee abundance and diversity in suburban yards. Biological Conservation 221:160–174.

Li F, Wang R, Paulussen J, Liu X. 2005. Comprehensive concept planning of urban greening based on ecological principles: a case study in Beijing, China. *Landscape and Urban Planning* 72(4):325–336.

Li W, Saphores J-DM, Gillespie TW. 2015. A comparison of the economic benefits of urban greenspaces estimated with NDVI and with high-resolution land cover data. *Landscape and Urban Planning* 133:105–117.

Lindenmayer DB, Welsh A, Donnelly C, Crane M, Michael D, Macgregor C, McBurney L, Montague-Drake R, Gibbons P. 2009. Are nest boxes a viable alternative source of cavities for hollow-dependent animals? Long-term monitoring of nest box occupancy, pest use and attrition. *Biological Conservation* 142(1):33–42.

Livesley SJ, McPherson GM, Calfapietra C. 2016. The urban forest and ecosystem services: impacts on urban water, heat, and pollution cycles at the tree, street, and city scale. *Journal of Environment Quality* 45(1):119.

Loeb SC, Post CJ, Hall ST. 2009. Relationship between urbanization and bat community structure in national parks of the southeastern U.S. *Urban Ecosystems* 12(2):197–214.

Löfvenhaft K, Björn C, Ihse M. 2002. Biotope patterns in urban areas: a conceptual model integrating biodiversity issues in spatial planning. *Landscape and Urban Planning* 58(2–4):223–240.

Longcore T, Rich C. 2004. Ecological light pollution. *Frontiers in Ecology and the Environment* 2(4).

Loss SR, Will T, Marra PP. 2013. The impact of free-ranging domestic cats on wildlife of the United States. *Nature Communications* 4(1).

Luber G, McGeehin M. 2008. Climate change and extreme heat events. *American Journal of Preventive Medicine* 35(5):429–435.

Lundholm JT, Richardson PJ. 2010. Habitat analogues for reconciliation ecology in urban and industrial environments: Habitat analogues. *Journal of Applied Ecology* 47(5):966–975.

Luniak M. 2004. Synurbization - adaptation of animal wildlife to urban development. :6.

Luz de la Maza C, Hernández J, Bown H, Rodríguez M, Escobedo F. 2002. Vegetation diversity in the Santiago de Chile urban ecosystem. *Arboricultural Journal* 26(4):347–357.

Lyford ME, Jackson ST, Betancourt JL, Gray ST. 2003. IInfluence of landscape structure and climate variability on a late Holocene plant migration. *Ecological Monographs* 73(4):567–583.

Major DC, Omojola A, Dettinger M, Hanson RT, Sanchez-Rodriguez R. 2011. Climate change, water, and wastewater in cities. In Rosenzweig C, Solecki WD, Hammer SA, Mehrotra S (eds), Climate Change and Cities, 113–144. Cambridge: Cambridge University Press.

Malanson GP. 2003. Dispersal across continuous and binary representations of landscapes. *Ecological Modelling* 169(1):17–24.

Matheson C. 1953. Some aspects of urban zoology in Great Britain. *The Scientific Monthly* 76(1):29–32.

Matsuba M, Nishijima S, Katoh K. 2016. Effectiveness of corridor vegetation depends on urbanization tolerance of forest birds in central Tokyo, Japan. *Urban Forestry & Urban Greening* 18:173–181.

Matthews SN, Rodewald PG. 2010. Urban forest patches and stopover duration of migratory Swainson's thrushes. *The Condor* 112(1):96–104.

McCleery RA, Moorman CE, Peterson MN. 2014. *Urban wildlife conservation: theory and practice*. Springer.

McFrederick QS, LeBuhn G. 2006. Are urban parks refuges for bumble bees Bombus spp. (Hymenoptera: Apidae)? *Biological Conservation* 129(3):372–382.

Mackenzie J, Haggerty S, Aguirre AC, Azumbrado T, Bruins J, Connolly D, Cortese D, Dutra-Vernaci C, Giacopini DM. 2017. Plan Bay Area 2040. Metropolitan Transportation Commission.

McKinney ML. 2002. Urbanization, Biodiversity, and Conservation. BioScience 52(10):883.

McKinney ML. 2006. Urbanization as a major cause of biotic homogenization. *Biological Conservation* 127(3):247–260.

McKinney ML. 2008. Effects of urbanization on species richness: a review of plants and animals. *Urban Ecosystems* 11(2):161–176.

McLachlan JS, Hellmann JJ, Schwartz MW. 2007. A framework for debate of assisted migration in an era of climate change. *Conservation Biology* 21(2):297–302.

Mclaughlin BC, Zavaleta ES. 2012. Predicting species responses to climate change: demography and climate microrefugia in California valley oak (Quercus lobata). *Global Change Biology* 18(7):2301–2312.

Meehl GA, Tebaldi C. 2004. More intense, more frequent, and longer lasting heat waves in the 21st Century. Science 305(5686):994–997.

Milligan MC, Dickinson JL. 2016. Habitat quality and nest-box occupancy by five species of oak woodland birds. *The Auk* 133(3):429–438.

Mitchell R, Popham F. 2008. Effect of exposure to natural environment on health inequalities: an observational population study. *The Lancet* 372(9650):1655–1660.

Morelli F, Beim M, Jerzak L, Jones D, Tryjanowski P. 2014. Can roads, railways and related structures have positive effects on birds? – A review. *Transportation Research Part D: Transport and Environment* 30:21–31.

Mumby PJ, Hastings A. 2007. The impact of ecosystem connectivity on coral reef resilience: coral reef resilence. *Journal of Applied Ecology* 45(3):854–862.

Munshi-South J, Kharchenko K. 2010. Rapid, pervasive genetic differentiation of urban white-footed mouse (Peromyscus leucopus) populations in New York City. *Molecular Ecology* 19(19):4242–4254.

Narango DL, Tallamy DW, Marra PP. 2018. Nonnative plants reduce population growth of an insectivorous bird. *Proceedings of the National Academy of Sciences* 115(45):11549–11554.

Nassauer JI, Wang Z, Dayrell E. 2009. What will the neighbors think? Cultural norms and ecological design. Landscape and Urban Planning 92(3–4):282–292.

Nielsen AB, van den Bosch M, Maruthaveeran S, van den Bosch CK. 2014. Species richness in urban parks and its drivers: a review of empirical evidence. *Urban Ecosystems* 17(1):305–327.

Nilon CH, Aronson MFJ, Cilliers SS, Dobbs C, Frazee LJ, Goddard MA, O'Neill KM, Roberts D, Stander EK, Werner P, et al. 2017. Planning for the future of urban biodiversity: a global review of city-scale initiatives. *BioScience* 67(4):332–342.

[NOAA] National Oceanic and Atmospheric Administration. 2019. San Francisco Bay Area/Monterey.

Nogués-Bravo D, Rodríguez-Sánchez F, Orsini L, de Boer E, Jansson R, Morlon H, Fordham DA, Jackson ST. 2018. Cracking the code of biodiversity responses to past climate change. *Trends in Ecology & Evolution* 33(10):765–776.

Norton BA, Evans KL, Warren PH. 2016. Urban biodiversity and landscape ecology: patterns, processes and planning. *Current Landscape Ecology Reports* 1(4):178–192.

Ogden LJE. 1996. Collision course: the hazards of lighted structures and windows to migrating birds. :53.

Ortega-welch M. 2018. Oakland's famous herons may be getting a new home. *Crosscurrents*.

Palma E, Catford JA, Corlett RT, Duncan RP, Hahs AK, McCarthy MA, McDonnell MJ, Thompson K, Williams NSG, Vesk PA. 2017. Functional trait changes in the floras of 11 cities across the globe in response to urbanization. Ecography 40(7):875–886.

Pardee GL, Philpott SM. 2014. Native plants are the bee's knees: local and landscape predictors of bee richness and abundance in backyard gardens. *Urban Ecosystems* 17(3):641–659.

Parra-Olea G, Wake D, Hammerson G. 2008. Aneides lugubris. The IUCN Red List of Threatened Species 2008: e.T59118A11884773. Accessed from http://dx.doi.org/10.2305/IUCN.UK.2008.RLTS.T59118A11884773.en, 2019-3-21.

Pecl GT, Araújo MB, Bell JD, Blanchard J, Bonebrake TC, Chen I-C, Clark TD, Colwell RK, Danielsen F, Evengård B, et al. 2017. Biodiversity redistribution under climate change: impacts on ecosystems and human well-being. *Science* 355(6332):eaai9214.

Pickett STA, Cadenasso ML, Grove JM, Boone CG, Groffman PM, Irwin E, Kaushal SS, Marshall V, McGrath BP, Nilon CH, et al. 2010. Urban ecological systems: scientific foundations and a decade of progress. Journal of Environmental Management 92 (2011): 331-362.

Plieninger T, Bieling C, Fagerholm N, Byg A, Hartel T, Hurley P, López-Santiago CA, Nagabhatla N, Oteros-Rozas E, Raymond CM, et al. 2015. The role of cultural ecosystem services in landscape management and planning. *Current Opinion in Environmental Sustainability* 14:28–33.

Poot H, Ens BJ, de Vries H, Donners MAH, Wernand MR, Marquenie JM. 2008. Green light for nocturnally migrating birds. *Ecology and Society* 13(2).

Rastandeh A, Pedersen Zari M. 2018. A spatial analysis of land cover patterns and its implications for urban avifauna persistence under climate change. *Landscape Ecology* 33(3):455–474.

Raupp MJ, Shrewsbury PM, Herms DA. 2010. Ecology of Herbivorous Arthropods in Urban Landscapes. Annual Review of Entomology 55(1):19–38.

Remacha C, Delgado JA. 2009. Spatial nest-box selection of cavity-nesting bird species in response to proximity to recreational infrastructures. *Landscape and Urban Planning* 93(1):46–53.

Riley SPD, Pollinger JP, Sauvajot RM, York EC, Bromley C, Fuller TK, Wayne RK. 2006. A southern California freeway is a physical and social barrier to gene flow in carnivores. *Molecular Ecology* 15(7):1733–1741.

Riley SPD, Sauvajot RM, Fuller TK, York EC, Kamradt DA, Bromley C, Wayne RK. 2003. Effects of urbanization and habitat fragmentation on bobcats and coyotes in southern California. *Conservation Biology* 17(2):566–576.

Robinson GR, Yurlina ME, Handel SN. 1994. A century of change in the Staten Island flora: ecological correlates of species losses and invasions. *Bulletin of the Torrey Botanical Club* 121(2):119.

Rodewald AD, Gehrt SD. 2014. Wildlife population dynamics in urban landscapes. In McCleery RA, Moorman CE, Peterson MN (eds), Urban Wildlife, 117–147. Boston, MA: Springer US.

Roman LA, Scatena FN. 2011. Street tree survival rates: meta-analysis of previous studies and application to a field survey in Philadelphia, PA, USA. *Urban Forestry & Urban Greening* 10(4):269–274

Rondinini C, Doncaster CP. 2002. Roads as barriers to movement for hedgehogs. *Functional Ecology* 16(4)504–509.

Van Rossum F, Triest L. 2012. Stepping-stone populations in linear landscape elements increase pollen dispersal between urban forest fragments. Plant Ecology and Evolution 145(3):332–340.

Rottenborn SC. 1999. Predicting the impacts of urbanization on riparian bird communities. *Biological Conservation* 88(3):289–299.

Samara Group LLC. n.d. Welcome to the Urban Biodiversity Inventory Framework [UBIF] Online Tool. 2013-2-28.

San Francisco Bay Regional Water Quality Control Board. 2004. Local Government Riparian Buffers in the San Francisco Bay Area.

Sandifer PA, Sutton-Grier AE, Ward BP. 2015. Exploring connections among nature, biodiversity, ecosystem services, and human health and well-being: Opportunities to enhance health and biodiversity conservation. *Ecosystem Services* 12:1–15.

Sandström UG, Angelstam P, Khakee A. 2006. Urban comprehensive planning – identifying barriers for the maintenance of functional habitat networks. *Landscape and Urban Planning* 75(1–2)43–57.

Santa Clara Valley Open Space Authority, Conservation Biology Institute. 2017. Coyote Valley landscape linkage: a vision for a resilient, multi-benefit landscape.

Satterfield DA, Villablanca FX, Maerz JC, Altizer S. 2016. Migratory monarchs wintering in California experience low infection risk compared to monarchs breeding year-round on non-native milkweed. *Integrative and Comparative Biology* 56(2):343–352.

Sawyer J, Keeler-Wolf T, Evens J. 2009. A manual of California vegetation. Second Edition. California Native Plant Society, Sacramento, CA USA.

Schwartz MW, Thorne JH, Viers JH. 2006. Biotic homogenization of the California flora in urban and urbanizing regions. *Biological Conservation* 127(3):282–291.

Schwarz K, Fragkias M, Boone CG, Zhou W, McHale M, Grove JM, O'Neil-Dunne J, McFadden JP, Buckley GL, Childers D, et al. 2015. Trees Grow on Money: Urban Tree Canopy Cover and Environmental Justice. *PLoS ONE* 10(4):e0122051.

Sears MK, Hellmich RL, Stanley-Horn DE, Oberhauser KS, Pleasants JM, Mattila HR, Siegfried BD, Dively GP. 2001. Impact of Bt corn pollen on monarch butterfly populations: A risk assessment. *Proceedings of the National Academy of Sciences* 98(21):11937–11942.

Sedgwick JA. 2000. Willow Flycatcher (Empidonax traillii). *The Birds of North America Online*.

Seewagen CL, Slayton EJ, Guglielmo CG. 2010. Passerine migrant stopover duration and spatial behaviour at an urban stopover site. *Acta Oecologica* 36(5):484–492.

[SF Environment] Board of Supervisors Unanimously Approve Resolution to Make Protecting Biodiversity a Citywide Priority. 2018. .

Shanahan DF, Miller C, Possingham HP, Fuller RA. 2011. The influence of patch area and connectivity on avian communities in urban revegetation. *Biological Conservation* 144(2):722–729.

Shochat E, Lerman SB, Anderies JM, Warren PS, Faeth SH, Nilon CH. 2010. Invasion, Competition, and Biodiversity Loss in Urban Ecosystems. *BioScience* 60(3):199–208.

Shochat E, Warren P, Faeth S, Mcintyre N, Hope D. 2006. From patterns to emerging processes in mechanistic urban ecology. *Trends in Ecology & Evolution* 21(4):186–191.

Shwartz A, Muratet A, Simon L, Julliard R. 2013. Local and management variables outweigh landscape effects in enhancing the diversity of different taxa in a big metropolis. *Biological Conservation* 157:285–292.

Shwartz A, Turbé A, Simon L, Julliard R. 2014. Enhancing urban biodiversity and its influence on city-dwellers: An experiment. Biological Conservation 171:82–90.

Smith CS, Gittman RK, Neylan IP, Scyphers SB, Morton JP, Joel Fodrie F, Grabowski JH, Peterson CH. 2017. Hurricane damage along natural and hardened estuarine shorelines: Using homeowner experiences to promote nature-based coastal protection. *Marine Policy* 81:350–358.

Smith LS, Fellowes MDE. 2014. The grass-free lawn: Management and species choice for optimum ground cover and plant diversity. *Urban Forestry & Urban Greening* 13(3):433–442.

Soga M, Yamaura Y, Koike S, Gaston KJ. 2014. Woodland remnants as an urban wildlife refuge: a cross-taxonomic assessment. *Biodiversity and Conservation* 23(3):649–659.

Sol D, González-Lagos C, Moreira D, Maspons J, Lapiedra O. 2014. Urbanisation tolerance and the loss of avian diversity. *Ecology letters* 17(8):942–950.

Soule ME, Bolger DT, Alberts AC, Wrights J, Sorice M, Hill S. 1988. Reconstructed Dynamics of Rapid Extinctions of Chaparral-Requiring Birds in Urban Habitat Islands. *Conservation Biology* 2(1):75–92.

Soulsbury CD, White PCL. 2015. Human–wildlife interactions in urban areas: a review of conflicts, benefits and opportunities. Wildlife Research 42(7):541.

Spear JE, Grijalva EK, Michaels JS, Parker SS. 2018. Ecological spillover dynamics of organisms from urban to natural landscapes. *Journal of Urban Ecology* 4(1).

Spotswood E, Grossinger R, Hagerty S, Beller E, Grenier JL, Askevold R. 2017. Re-Oaking Silicon Valley: Building Vibrant Cities with Nature.

Stacey PB, Taper M. 1992. Environmental Variation and the Persistence of Small Populations. *Ecological Applications* 2(1):18–29.

Stagoll K, Lindenmayer DB, Knight E, Fischer J, Manning AD. 2012. Large trees are keystone structures in urban parks: Urban keystone structures. *Conservation Letters* 5(2):115–122.

Standish RJ, Hobbs RJ, Miller JR. 2013. Improving city life: options for ecological restoration in urban landscapes and how these might influence interactions between people and nature. *Landscape Ecology* 28(6):1213–1221.

Stone GN, Hernandez-Lopez A, Nicholls JA, di Pierro E, Pujade-Villar J, Melika G, Cook JM. 2009. Extreme host plant conservatism during at least 20 million years of host plant pursuit by oak gal wasps. *Evolution* 63(4):854–869.

Strauss SY, Lau JA, Carroll SP. 2006. Evolutionary responses of natives to introduced species: what do introductions tell us about natural communities?: Evolutionary responses of natives to introduced species. *Ecology Letters* 9(3):357–374.

Tan J, Zheng Y, Tang X, Guo C, Li L, Song G, Zhen X, Yuan D, Kalkstein AJ, Li F, et al. 2010. The urban heat island and its impact on heat waves and human health in Shanghai. International Journal of Biometeorology 54(1):75–84.

Tershy B, Harrison S, Borker A, Sinervo B, Cornelisse T, Li C, Spatz D, Croll D, Zavaleta E. 2016. Biodiversity. Ecosystems of California. University of California Press.

Tewksbury JJ, Levey DJ, Haddad NM, Sargent S, Orrock JL, Weldon A, Danielson BJ, Brinkerhoff J, Damschen EI, Townsend P. 2002. Corridors affect plants, animals, and their interactions in fragmented landscapes. *Proceedings of the National Academy of Sciences* 99(20):12923–12926.

Tews J, Brose U, Grimm V, Tielbörger K, Wichmann MC, Schwager M, Jeltsch F. 2004. Animal species diversity driven by habitat heterogeneity/diversity. *Journal of Biogeography* 31(1):79–92.

Thomas A, Gill RA. 2017. Patterns of urban forest composition in Utah's growing mountain communities. *Urban Forestry & Urban Greening* 23:104–112.

Threlfall CG, Mata L, Mackie JA, Hahs AK, Stork NE, Williams NSG, Livesley SJ. 2017. Increasing biodiversity in urban greenspaces through simple vegetation interventions. *Journal of Applied Ecology* 54(6):1874–1883.

Thrush SF, Halliday J, Hewitt JE, Lohrer AM. 2008. The effects of habitat loss, fragmentation, and community homogenization on resilience in estuaries. *Ecological Applications* 18(1):12–21.

Tigas LA, Van Vuren DH, Sauvajot RM. 2002. Behavioral responses of bobcats and coyotes to habitat fragmentation and corridors in an urban environment. *Biological Conservation* 108(3):299–306.

Tonietto R, Fant J, Ascher J, Ellis K, Larkin D. 2011. A comparison of bee communities of Chicago green roofs, parks and prairies. *Landscape and Urban Planning* 103(1):102–108.

Tremblay J, Ellison L. 1979. Effects of human disturbance on breeding of black-crowned night herons. *The Auk* 96(2).

Tremblay MA, St. Clair CC. 2009. Factors affecting the permeability of transportation and riparian corridors to the movements of songbirds in an urban landscape. Journal of Applied Ecology.

Tremblay MA, St. Clair CC. 2011. Permeability of a heterogeneous urban landscape to the movements of forest songbirds: songbird movements in urban landscapes. *Journal of Applied Ecology* 48(3):679–688.

Tscharntke T, Tylianakis JM, Rand TA, Didham RK, Fahrig L, Batáry P, Bengtsson J, Clough Y, Crist TO, Dormann CF, et al. 2012. Landscape moderation of biodiversity patterns and processes - eight hypotheses. *Biological Reviews* 87(3):661–685.

Ürge-Vorsatz D, Rosenzweig C, Dawson RJ, Sanchez Rodriguez R, Bai X, Barau AS, Seto KC, Dhakal S. 2018. Locking in positive climate responses in cities. *Nature Climate Change* 8(3):174–177.

US Census Bureau. 2016. Geo time series, TIGER/Line Shapefiles.

[USFS] United States Forest Service, United States Department of Agriculture. n.d. Monarch butterfly habitat needs. 2019-2-28.

[USGS] United States Geological Survey. 1899. San Jose topographic quadrangle.

[USGS] United States Geological Survey. 2010. Urban Dynamics: Temporal Urban Mapping. USGS Land Cover Institute.

van den Berg M, Wendel-Vos W, van Poppel M, Kemper H, van Mechelen W, Maas J. 2015. Health benefits of greenspaces in the living environment: a systematic review of epidemiological studies. Urban Forestry & Urban Greening 14(4):806–816.

van Heezik YM, Dickinson KJM, Freeman C. 2012. Closing the gap: communicating to change gardening practices in support of native biodiversity in urban private gardens. Ecology and Society 17(1).

Van Rossum F, Triest L. 2012. Stepping-stone populations in linear landscape elements increase pollen dispersal between urban forest fragments. *Plant Ecology and Evolution* 145(3):332–340.

Vergnes A, Viol IL, Clergeau P. 2012. Green corridors in urban landscapes affect the arthropod communities of domestic gardens. *Biological Conservation* :10.

Wang R, Ateljevich E. 2012. A Continuous Surface Elevation Map for Modeling (Chapter 6). In Methodology for Flow and Salinity Estimates in the Sacramento-San Joaquin Delta and Suisun Mars, 23rd Annual Progress Report to the State Water Resources Control Board. California Department of Water Resources, Bay-Delta Office, Delta Modeling Section.

Warren PS, Harlan SL, Boone C, Lerman SB, Shochat E, Kinzig AP. 2010. Urban ecology and human social organisation. In Gaston KJ (ed), Urban Ecology, 172–201. Cambridge: Cambridge University Press.

Weaver LA, Garman GC. 1994. Urbanization of a watershed and historical changes in a stream fish assemblage. *Transactions of the American Fisheries Society* 123(2):162–172.

Whitburn J, Linklater WL, Milfont TL. 2018. Exposure to urban nature and tree planting are related to pro-environmental behavior via connection to nature, the use of nature for psychological restoration, and environmental attitudes. Environment and Behavior :0013916517751100.

Whited D, Galatowitsch S, Tester JR, Schik K, Lehtinen R, Husveth J. 2000. The importance of local and regional factors in predicting effective conservation planning strategies for wetland bird communities in agricultural and urban landscapes. *Landscape and Urban Planning* :17.

Williams NSG, Schwartz MW, Vesk PA, McCarthy MA, Hahs AK, Clemants SE, Corlett RT, Duncan RP, Norton BA, Thompson K, et al. 2009. A conceptual framework for predicting the effects of urban environments on floras. *Journal of Ecology* 97(1):4–9.

Wolfe BE, Rodgers VL, Stinson KA, Pringle A. 2008. The invasive plant Alliaria petiolata (garlic mustard) inhibits ectomycorrhizal fungi in its introduced range. Journal of Ecology 96(4):777–783.

Wolf KM, DiTomaso JM. 2016. Management of blue gum eucalyptus in California requires region-specific consideration. *California Agriculture* 70(1):39–47.

Wratten SD, Gillespie M, Decourtye A, Mader E, Desneux N. 2012. Pollinator habitat enhancement: benefits to other ecosystem services. *Agriculture, Ecosystems & Environment* 159:112–122.

Wu J. 2014. Urban ecology and sustainability: The state-of-the-science and future directions. *Landscape and Urban Planning* 125:209–221.

Zeiner D, Laudenslayer, Jr. W, Mayer K, White M. 1988. California's wildlife. Accessed from https://www.wildlife.ca.gov/Data/CWHR/Life-History-and-Range, 2019-2-28.

Zipperer WC, Foresman TW, Walker SP, Daniel CT. 2012. Ecological consequences of fragmentation and deforestation in an urban landscape: a case study. *Urban Ecosystems* 15(3):533–544.

Ziter C. 2016. The biodiversity-ecosystem service relationship in urban areas: a quantitative review. *Oikos* 125(6):761–768.

APPENDICES

Appendix A

CASE STUDY: SILICON VALLEY

Study Area

The study area included in the Silicon Valley case study (Chapter 3, Fig. 3.1 and all subsequent maps) includes the urbanized area between Coyote Creek and San Francisquito Creeks, as well as all the creeks in between that drain to the San Francisco Bay. The study area mostly follows the urbanized footprint of Santa Clara County, though some of Morgan Hill to the south is excluded (based on a watershed boundary), and East Palo Alto to the north is included (this city lies in San Mateo County). The northern boundary also excludes the tidal marshes and salt ponds in the San Francisco Bay. This boundary was digitized manually, and lies within the city limits of various municipalities. Small discontiguous urban areas in the hills were also manually excluded.

Data used to create this study area include the 2010 USGS Urban Dynamics Data Set (built-up lands in the San Francisco Bay region) as the urban template. Additionally, we relied on data from the Santa Clara Valley Water District (SCVWD) to determine watershed boundaries. In addition, the land use map in Figure 3.2 was reclassified from over 100 land use types from the Association of Bay Area Governments (ABAG 2006).

Patch size

Maps and analyses in this element (Fig. 3.3 and 3.4) were created from the California Protected Area Database (CPAD) and the California Conservation Easement Database (CCED) data, which together represent lands owned in fee or protected for open space purposes by public agencies or non-profits (CPAD 2017a and CCED 2016). While other private or unindexed open spaces may exist, these layers serve as a baseline of existing public or non-profit owned or protected lands, and includes most publicly accessible open spaces. In some cases, adjacent parcels were merged so that parks bordering one another were considered a single habitat patch. In addition, other small adjustments to boundaries were made around river corridors and city parks where land cover suggested a coherent patch that extended slightly beyond property boundaries. For example, the many individual parcels that comprise Guadalupe River Park were merged where there were no large gaps between parcels.

Connections

The map (Silicon Valley Connections: Stream Corridors) and analysis (Habitat Connectivity of Silicon Valley Waterways) in Figures 3.6 and 3.7 relied on Bay Area Aquatic Resources Inventory (BAARI), version 2.1 2017 (SFEI), and riparian survey data acquired from SCVWD's 2010 Stream Maintenance Renewal Project (surveys performed by Aerial Information Systems [AIS 2010]). Data represents dominant vegetation community structure at a given data point, down to species composition.

Waterways were classified as underground or above-ground based on BAARI data. Waterways within BAARI classifications "fluvial channel", "fluvial ditch", and "fluvial engineered channel" were categorized as above-ground, while "fluvial subsurface drainages" were categorized as underground. Above-ground waterways were further classified as "vegetated," "unvegetated," or "no data" based on the SCVWD dataset. Waterways were labeled as "unvegetated" when they overlapped with SCVWD vegetation type categories "areas of little or no vegetation group," "built up & urban disturbance group," "concrete lined channels," "earth lined channels," "perennial stream channel," "reservoirs," "river & lacustrine flats & streambeds," "roads > 50 ft wide," or "water group." Waterways were classified as "no data" when they fell outside of the SCVWD survey extent or overlapped with the SCVWD category "unknown type group (flagged for field)." All other above-ground waterways were categorized as "vegetated."

Matrix quality

The map and analysis of canopy cover in Figures 3.9 and 3.10 used data acquired from CalFire's Urban and Community Forestry program, which describes their methods as follows: *"an urban tree canopy baseline was compiled from the existing California tree inventories, databases, and combined with data from a new 1-meter resolution map product of tree canopy, from EarthDefine (2013). EarthDefine data is based on 2012 NAIP imagery."* These data were averaged to produce a final layer with a resolution of 30 × 30 meters. Additional information on methods used to produce the CalFire layer can be found in Bjorkman et al. 2015.

Habitat diversity

Santa Clara Valley Historical Habitat types represented in Figure 3.12 is a combination of mapping efforts from multiple San Francisco Estuary Institute historical ecology reports (Grossinger et al. 2006, Grossinger et al. 2008, Beller et al. 2010). Some habitat types were grouped for simplicity. For example, "Alkali meadow" includes high and low concentration alkali meadow types; "Shallow Water" includes shallow bay and shallow tidal channel; "Tidal flat" includes tidal flat / channel and tidal marsh panne.

The "Palo Alto Oaks and Historical Wet Meadow" diagram (Figure 3.13), used a comprehensive survey of all oaks in Palo Alto from the OakWell Survey conducted by Canopy (Canopy 2003). The density map was created using a point density analysis, which calculated the number of oak trees within a 500 foot buffer of each tree in the dataset. The historical wet meadow overlay was based on SFEI historical ecology studies described above.

Native vegetation

The map of Silicon Valley Native Vegetation (Figure 3.16) and analyses in Figure 3.15 were based on street tree inventory data from various cities, vegetation classifications from CalVeg, and riparian stream surveys from SCVWD (AIS 2010).

Street tree inventory data

Street tree inventory data includes the cities of Palo Alto and East Palo Alto and Mountain View, Cupertino, and San Jose. These datasets are available to the public, and most can be accessed through online GIS data portals on the websites for each city. Street tree inventory data include only municipally owned and managed trees, and exclude all privately owned trees. Therefore, inventories do not fully represent the population of trees in the urban landscape and underestimate the overall tree density in the area. Because surveys are conducted by individual cities, are not mandated, many cities do not have comprehensive inventories of street trees. Thus, our dataset contains large gaps; data was not available for Santa Clara, Campbell, Alviso, or Sunnyvale. Each inventory was standardized, and species names were made consistent (including managing synonyms and misspellings). Vacant sites and incomplete records were dropped from the dataset.

> Identifying native trees. Trees were considered native if they were historically native to the Santa Clara Valley floor. Note that because the emphasis was on trees native to the valley floor, this list does not include other common street trees native to the region at a higher elevation or in a more moist climate, such as *Sequoia sempervirens*, or trees native likely to other parts of California, such as *Cercis occidentalis*.

> Native trees were identified using a variety of sources, including *Terrestrial Vegetation of California* (Barbour et al. 2007); the Holland Classifications from the *Manual of California Vegetation* (Sawyer et al. 2009); historical ecology data (Grossinger et al. 2006, Grossinger et al. 2008, Beller et al. 2010); *The Distribution of Forest Trees in California* (Griffin and Critchfield 1972); CalFlora (https://www.calflora.org/); and the California Native Plant Society's CalScape tool (https://calscape.org/).

> **Classified as native:** *Acer macrophyllum, Acer negundo, Aesculus californica, Alnus rhombifolia, Heteromeles arbutifolia, Platanus racemosa, Populus fremontii, Prunus ilicifolia, Quercus agrifolia, Quercus douglasii, Quercus kelloggii, Quercus lobata, Sambucus caerulea, Sambucus mexicana,* and *Umbellularia californica*.

CALVEG

This dataset represents modern habitat vegetation classifications, using a modified version of data from CALVEG. CALVEG is a USDA Forest Service product providing a comprehensive spatial dataset of existing vegetation cover across the state of California. The data were created using a combination of remote sensing classification, photo editing, and field based observations. More information on CALVEG can be found here: http://www.fs.usda.gov/detail/r5/landmanagement/resourcemanagement/?cid=stelprdb5347192.

This particular layer was acquired from the Conservation Lands Network (CLN) of the Bay Area Open Space Council, and is a modified version of original CALVEG data. Details how the Council's version differs from the original are described here: https://www.bayarealands.org/explorer/glossary/vegetation.html. The analysis of native and non-native vegetation included only vegetation classifications, excluding water, rock, and urban classification types. Data represents dominant vegetation community structure. Vegetation was classified as follows:

> **Classified as native:** Blue Oak Forest / Woodland, California Bay Forest, Central Coast Riparian Forests, Coastal Salt Marsh / Coastal Brackish Marsh, Coastal

Scrub, Mixed Montane Chaparral, Montane Hardwoods, Permanent Freshwater Marsh, Redwood Forest, Semi-Desert Scrub / Desert Scrub, Serpentine Barren, Serpentine Grassland, Serpentine Hardwoods, Serpentine Riparian, Chamise Chaparral, Coast Live Oak Forest / Woodland, Valley Oak Forest / Woodland

Classified as non-native: Non-Native Ornamental Conifer-Hardwood Mixture, Non-native/Ornamental Grass, Cultivated, Moderate grasslands, Warm grasslands

Riparian stream surveys.

Vegetation types from SCVWD were classified into native, non-native and other vegetation (this class was not mapped) classes. All built and water classifications were excluded from the analysis, including built/urban, channels, reservoirs, rivers and streambeds, and roads. Vegetation was classified as follows:

Classified as native: *Acer negundo, Aesculus californica, Alnus rhombifolia,* Areas of Little or No Vegetation Group, Arid Freshwater Emergent Marsh Group (Marsh vegetation), *Artemisia californica, Baccharis pilularis,* Bulrush - Cattail mapping unit, California Perennial & Annual Grasslands Mapping Unit Group (Native component), Chord Grass, Fresh or brackish Bulrush spp. mapping unit, *Juglans hindsii* Semi-Natural Stands, *Platanus racemosa, Populus fremontii, Quercus agrifolia, Quercus lobata, Salicornia* - Salt Grass - *Jaumea, Salix exigua, Salix laevigata, Sambucus nigra* (lumped with Mexican elderberry), Serpentine Component Mapping Unit, Southwestern North American Riparian Evergreen & Deciduous Woodlands Group

Classified as non-native: *Arundo donax, Conium-Foeniculum* patches, Eucalyptus, Exotic Trees (Canopy Height <2 Meters), Exotic Trees (Canopy Height >15 Meters), Exotic Trees, (Canopy Height 2-15 Meters), *Lepidium latifolium,* Mediterranean California Naturalized Annual & Perennial Grassland Group (Weedy grasslands with no native component - Ruderal), Orchards, *Rubus discolor, Sequoia sempervirens*

Special resources

The map and analysis of Special Resources (Figs. 3.18 and 3.19) was based on street tree inventories, used to identify large trees and the Bay Area Aquatic Resources Inventory, used to identify the locations and sizes of wetlands and streams (BAARI version 2.1, SFEI 2017). See Connections and Native Plants sections above for descriptions of these datasets. Figure 2.18, showing the distribution of native and non-native trees by size, excluded Palo Alto and East Palo Alto, because these cities did not include diameter information for very large trees.

Other basemaps

Other maps included throughout chapter 3 include a digital elevation model the Department of Water Resources (Wang and Ateljevich 2012) and TIGER/Line Shapefile roads courtesy of the US Census Bureau (2016).

Appendix B

LIST OF KEY PAPERS USED IN DEVELOPING ELEMENTS

1. Beninde J, Veith M, Hochkirch A. 2015. Biodiversity in cities needs space: a meta-analysis of factors determining intra-urban biodiversity variation. Ecology Letters 18(6):581–592.

2. Aronson MFJ, La Sorte FA, Nilon CH, Katti M, Goddard MA, Lepczyk CA, Warren PS, Williams NSG, Cilliers S, Clarkson B, et al. 2014. A global analysis of the impacts of urbanization on bird and plant diversity reveals key anthropogenic drivers. Proceedings of the Royal Society B: Biological Sciences 281(1780):20133330–20133330.

3. Aronson MF, Lepczyk CA, Evans KL, Goddard MA, Lerman SB, MacIvor JS, Nilon CH, Vargo T. 2017. Biodiversity in the city: key challenges for urban greenspace management. Frontiers in Ecology and the Environment 15(4):189–196.

4. Aronson MFJ, Nilon CH, Lepczyk CA, Parker TS, Warren PS, Cilliers SS, Goddard MA, Hahs AK, Herzog C, Katti M, et al. 2016. Hierarchical filters determine community assembly of urban species pools. Ecology 97(11):2952–2963.

5. Goddard MA, Dougill AJ, Benton TG. 2010. Scaling up from gardens: biodiversity conservation in urban environments. Trends in Ecology & Evolution 25(2):90–98.

6. Goddard MA, Ikin K, Lerman SB. 2017. Ecological and social factors determining the diversity of birds in residential yards and gardens. In Murgui E, Hedblom M (eds), Ecology and Conservation of Birds in Urban Environments, 371–397. Cham: Springer International Publishing.

7. Bateman PW, Fleming PA. 2012. Big city life: carnivores in urban environments. Journal of Zoology 287(1):1–23.

8. Raupp MJ, Shrewsbury PM, Herms DA. 2010. Ecology of herbivorous arthropods in urban landscapes. Annual Review of Entomology 55(1):19–38.

9. Norton BA, Evans KL, Warren PH. 2016. Urban biodiversity and landscape ecology: patterns, processes and planning. Current Landscape Ecology Reports 1(4):178–192.